# WRITING
# SHORT
# STORY

## A Hands-On
## Program

# ABOUT THE AUTHOR

Jack M. Bickham published more than seventy-five novels after getting his start with short stories in the science-fiction and western fields. Also a longtime teacher, he wrote extensively about the craft of fiction. His titles for Writer's Digest Books are *Scene and Structure* and *Setting*.

# WRITING the SHORT STORY

## A Hands-On Program

**Jack M. Bickham**

**WRITER'S DIGEST BOOKS**
Cincinnati, Ohio

This book is based upon a series that appeared in *Writer's Digest* magazine.

Other fine Writer's Digest Books are available from your local bookstore or direct from the publisher.

02  01  00  99  98      5  4  3  2  1

**Library of Congress Cataloging-in-Publication Data**

Bickham, Jack M.
     Writing the short story / Jack M. Bickham.—1st ed.
         p.     cm.
     Includes index.
     ISBN 0-89879-880-9 (pbk.: alk.paper)
     1. Fiction—Technique.   2. Short story.   I. Title.
PN3373.B45    1994
808.3'1—dc20                                                94-29207
                                                              CIP

Edited by Jack Heffron
Interior design by Brian Roeth
Cover design by Paul Neff

# ACKNOWLEDGMENTS

I owe special thanks to the many writers who responded to my earlier series on short story writing in *Writer's Digest* magazine. Without their feedback, this enhanced and expanded presentation might not have been possible. Also — as always — my appreciation to editor Jack Heffron, whose eagle eye caught mistakes and suggested countless improvements.

# TABLE OF CONTENTS

## Chapter One

# Why This Book?

I f you've spent much time recently reading the modern short story—as I assume you have—you may be wondering how anyone could dare to write a book suggesting a practical, hands-on approach to writing tales of this type for today's marketplace.

The contemporary short story, as you probably realize, most often appears to be *terra incognita*, an unknown land that sometimes shows features you've never seen before—without evident rules or consistency, with a form that seems to change in no apparent pattern, without the kind of logical consistency that a step-by-step approach implies.

In truth, much of the seeming confusion about the short story today is illusory. The principles that made a good story a century ago are largely still in force today. It is not unknown territory after all; it can be mapped in such a way that you can find road directions at every turn, and by following all the "route signs," learn to produce much finer and more satisfying short fiction.

It's true that the short story as usually published today *seems* to lack much of the classic form and plot content that used to characterize it. Often it's harder to find the beginning, middle and end of a short story, or to guess what the editors may want next. But, again, much of this apparent chaos is an illusion. The things that made a good story long ago still make a good story today.

Further, there are distinct advantages for you in knowing classic short story form, and how to apply it for today's readers. Without such mental guidelines — without such an internal "map" telling her what a story ought to be — a writer is left to depend solely on the most felicitous combination of writing style, characters, setting and mood. Sometimes the idea for such a short story, held together by feeling, may come to you. And you may find a home for it in a magazine somewhere.

But that method is such an iffy proposition.

Sure, maybe with enough talent and luck you may sell a short story now and then strictly on the basis of a momentary inspiration, and without any idea what you're doing. But inspiration for such stories does not come every day. Also, they usually must be written in the heat of the inspiration, a work-method that often involves exhausting weekends punctuated by long periods when you don't have idea number one, and must miserably wait for the next inspiration because you don't know how to think about "story" or find ideas for them.

You can't build a career on such hit-or-miss inspiration alone.

Your work will be more consistent and lucrative if you understand what you're doing, even if at times you know the classic pattern and decide to deviate from it for good reasons.

By gaining a knowledge of classic short story form and by following the procedures outlined in this book, you can avoid the lost feeling that often characterizes waiting for inspiration or writing without a plan. You will write with less fear and more confidence.

There may be a few of you out there who get an uneasy feeling at this point when I speak of classic story form or an organized pattern of work. I well remember the time, many years ago, when I graduated from a traditional English department and then met my first successful fiction writer. In college I had subscribed to the idea, still prevalent here and there in the land, that the creation of fiction is a mysterious process, an accident based on an act of God or some elusive muse; this concept of how "good" writers write carried along with it the unexamined assumption that "good" fiction could be produced only by inspiration or magic, and that you somehow cheapened the whole creative process if you tried too hard to analyze it.

It just isn't true. Virtually all successful writers carry around their own "map" of fiction in their head. Your map may not be exactly like mine in all details, and mine may not be exactly like Stephen King's, but by the time you finish this book we will all be on the same page of the atlas, agreeing on a tremendously high percentage of concepts about what makes a short story tick.

So I hope you can abandon the "magic inspiration theory" if ever you held to it. Here in our step-by-step approach to creating short fiction we will be taking a position quite the opposite of the inspiration idea. We'll be laying out a blueprint for work—a map, as I'll often call it—which will allow inspiration to work when it comes, but allow you to work and write good stories whether or not inspiration has recently struck.

Further, even when inspiration does strike, driving you to write a story almost blindly, your knowledge of the classic assumptions of the short story writer—and having a systematic approach to your work—can't possibly hurt you. It may even help with revision of the most "inspired" story, written largely from instinct.

Finally, it should be noted that few short story writers go through a career without at least once assaying a longer fiction form—the novella or the novel. The methods offered here make for more effective short fiction, but they work equally well with longer forms where inspiration and hopeful ambiguity will *not* be acceptable either as a work pattern or as a formless "form" in the finished work.

## WHO CAN THIS BOOK HELP?

Obviously I believe this book can help any number of people. You might fit one or more of the following profiles of intended readers.

**You don't want to wait for inspiration.** As noted above, inspiration may not come often enough to give you sufficient output or confidence for building a career in writing. If you follow this book's map, you will have a work attitude, and a system, that will help you develop ideas virtually on demand.

Unless you are an old and weary writer of fiction, you may not quite realize how important this is. There are times in every writer's life when she wants to write, but can't seem to come up with an idea. The Map will not only show you how to write clear and engaging short fiction *today*; it will provide you with a backlog of story ideas and materials into which you can dip at any time for a new story, without waiting for a moment of creative magic.

**Your inspiration or ideas have run dry.** Even the best writers sometimes find their story and story development ideas lifeless and uninteresting. This is often a sign of fatigue or temporary burnout. The procedures in this book will give you a new way of approaching your work, and refreshing and focusing your creative energies.

Even if you will trust the process outlined here in the Map, you may still suffer sometimes from discouragement or fatigue. Those, too, are an unfortunate part of the writer's life. But you will always have a system to fall back upon, and materials on which you can work.

**You're just starting out.** If this is the case, you may save years of lonely rejection and learning the hard way — from costly and discouraging mistakes. Herein you will find a methodology that will give you insights and good working habits right from the start.

Here again the Map removes magical, mystical elements from the creative writing process, replacing them with a balanced and logical system for your guidance. If at times you choose to deviate from the procedures given here, you will do so with full knowledge of the norm, and why you may be deviating from it.

Many writers take years learning by trial and error — writing and rejection. You have every reason to hope that the Map will drastically shorten that learning time.

**You're doing OK, but want to improve.** Chances are strong that the Map procedures will, as mentioned above, give your creative production better focus; but the system outlined here will also help you analyze copy to improve yourself still further.

The key to improvement for many writers lies in such analysis. They learn how to analyze their own copy for weaknesses, and they learn how to analyze the work of published authors to learn from them.

Such analysis goes beyond examination of style or syntax. You can learn to take characters apart and see why they are effective — or how they can be made so. You will see the structure that underlies good short fiction, and you will learn research techniques to give your stories a sounder footing, as well as revision procedures to make your copy stronger.

In all of this, the key is knowing what questions to ask as you analyze fiction. The Map provides that guide.

**You want to be more consistent.** One story pleases you and the next one drives you crazy with frustration? Or one day you're writing well, and the next day you can't seem to "turn it on"? Consistency is a bonus in this writing system because you approach each creative effort with essentially the same criteria for excellence.

Note again, please, that we cannot hope to remove all frustration and inconsistency from our work. Even the greatest writers have been said to have produced unpublishable work. That's because every writer's production—no matter how systematically handled—still tends to fluctuate a bit in quality, depending on such uncontrollable matters as outside distractions and health. Understanding the Map, however, can raise the general quality of your work—the parameters of excellence within which your output may vary. If you now tend to vary between "poor" and "fair" in your output, the procedures in this book can raise your creative bracket to a range between "fair" and "good."

Or, we hope, between "good" and "outstanding!"

**You're considering a longer work.** Every idea presented in this book works equally well with longer projects. The Map is a practically foolproof way to plan a major work of perhaps 100,000 words, or even more.

A few months after an abbreviated version of this material appeared in *Writer's Digest* magazine as a series, I had a letter from a woman who had just sold her first novel. It was a fine sale indeed, and she told me how she used the Map procedures to outline her book. It was a long book: Her action sequence cards extended the length of a long hallway! But she stayed with the system, followed her map, and sold her book. Such successes are possible, given determination guided by a creative system.

No one can promise you great success in any endeavor. But I hope to have convinced you to read the following pages with care, *and to do every assignment as it is assigned.*

Doing the assignments is vital. You may find it necessary sometimes to stop in the middle of a chapter to do some work. By the end of most chapters you will have been given one or more assignments, and the point will be made often that you should not read the next chapter until you have completed the work already assigned.

The brief Progress Check sections at the top of chapters will serve to remind you of work that should be completed or ongoing.

Please don't skip assignments. They are at the heart of the step-by-step approach—the key to understanding all the details of your map to consistent, logical, moving short fiction.

Finally, you will notice that this book deviates on four occasions from the normal progression of instructive chapters, with their specific assignments. These sections, called Time Out, deal with larger aspects of fiction than are considered in the step-by-step chapters. I hope they'll provide you with an occasional welcome respite from my infernal assignment making, and at the same time help you begin to synthesize your own "big picture" of how all fiction works.

Take your time, do all the assignments when asked to do so, control your impatience, and read the Time Out sections in a quest for the bigger picture. If you'll do these things, I can guarantee that by the end of the book you will have written at least one short story of the highest quality possible at your present level of development. Many who followed the shorter series in *Writer's Digest* reported getting the ideas for several new stories, and actually completing more than one before the series concluded. You may do the same.

Good luck!

*Chapter Two*

# How the Map Works

PROGRESS CHECK:

✔ *If you have not yet done so, make up your mind that you will* not *rush through the Map.*

✔ *Determine to take as much time as necessary for each assignment.*

✔ *Set up a preliminary work schedule.*

As the title of this book suggests, it's possible to take a logical, hands-on approach to writing the short story, rather than hoping good stories will emerge by luck. Here I offer you a detailed working plan—a map, as we called it before—that provides a detailed, comprehensive, logical, step-by-step method for imagining, creating and revising your short story. By taking you one step at a time, this map provides a method for learning the kind of thinking and the working principles that guide professional writers.

Each step contained herein is a building block. Step 4, for example, can be fully understood and used only after you have mastered steps 1, 2 and 3. This gives you the best-organized method for learning your craft at your own pace. At any time, if you begin to feel confused, go back to the place where you lost your way, and restudy before proceeding.

Note, please, that the Map's approach depends on your understanding of each block as it is presented. Often, full understanding will depend on practice of a given point. Therefore, the Map's effectiveness for you will depend not only on your absorption of material, but on your completion of all prescribed work.

Do you begin to get the idea that careful, systematic work through the Map is absolutely necessary if you are to derive maximum benefit? Good. Even so, the point is repeated often in the pages that follow. It's so easy to read some instructions, believe you already understand the point perfectly (and so don't need to do the assignment) or feel anxious to read further (and so can't spare the time to do the assignment). Yielding to either nonwork impulse is potentially destructive to the entire system. Patience!

In addition to the Progress Check sections that lead each chapter, other self-checks in the form of questions and examples will help you gauge your progress. The result: logical thinking about your story ideas, a logical framework for your imagination, and logical fiction that will make sense to readers, and appeal to them.

The Map may be worked through, beginning to end, in a relatively short period of time. But reading this book is not a speed exercise; if it takes weeks or months to finish your first *working* reading, there is no problem. As a matter of fact, the greatest danger to this book's effectiveness is your possible tendency to rush, skip or ignore instructions. Once more it must be emphasized: You must pause when told to do so, and do the work as outlined. Only in this way will you derive maximum benefit. The Map is not merely descriptive. It is a workbook.

I urge the use of $3'' \times 5''$ or $4'' \times 6''$ filing-type cards for the Map's organizational method. You may have a computer with something like Microsoft Windows, and be tempted to use that software's card-filing application. As useful as Windows and similar software systems may be for other applications, use the old-fashioned cards instead for this exercise.

Cards are preferred for a number of reasons, including the following.

Cards are portable in almost all circumstances. You can carry a few of them with you to the office, the grocery, the evening dinner, or even the bathtub. You will thus always have some with you to seize an idle moment and review ideas for a character you are having trouble with, for example, or jot down a sudden new idea that you might forget and lose forever if you were to wait until you could get home to your computer.

Having the cards with you at almost all times is a constant reminder of your work, and its seriousness. The simple act of carrying the cards will remind you that writing is not an on-again-off-again, hit-or-miss proposition, but a continuing, regular commitment.

The work of writing on your cards is a small physical effort, but even this small bit of physical labor can sometimes focus your thinking. As time goes by and you grow accustomed to the card system, you may indeed find that merely pulling out a card to jot a note helps focus your thinking more clearly. (I am not sure why this is so, but perhaps it has something to do with habit, and the mysterious way in which doing work repeatedly seems to make one better able to repeat the task in the future.)

Cards also have a distinct advantage in the ease with which they can be physically manipulated (i.e., moved around; arranged and rearranged on a desktop; or even taped in sequence on a worktable, along a wall, or across a room). You will find as you progress through the Map that you may often want to change your planned order of cards, insert new ones representing ideas as they occur, or pull out one and substitute another. While it's possible to do this on a computer, it tends to be more cumbersome.

Cards are *tactile*. You can shuffle them, move them between your fingers, scratch on them, even lose your temper and crumple some of them. This physical contact, too, may help your creativity in some mysterious way.

Cards can't "crash" like a computer hard disk may. They are not dependent on electricity or even on a battery. And once you've started creating and collecting them, they remain in view—they can't be hidden by your changing to a different directory, as they might be if you had them somewhere in the electronic innards of your computer.

Cards are a lot cheaper. I bought five hundred new 3″ × 5″ cards not long ago for the grand total of $1.80.

In addition to cards—lots of them—you will need a couple of other simple items for working with the Map. They are as follows.

Colored pencils. Six will do. These will be used for marking up copy. (My latest box is from Crayola, and includes a dozen colors. Again, being a tightwad, I appreciate that they cost $2.89.)

Two spiral or loose-leaf notebooks, preferably lined. One of these will be used as a working journal—a repository for ideas and observations about the work done by you and others—and the second will be used for compiling research notes, facts picked up on a field trip checking out a setting, perhaps, or observations you may have collected first on cards about a particular real-life person who may provide a basis for an interesting character.

It's assumed you have a computer with a good word processing program in it, or a good typewriter. Most professionals, even the most stubborn, have gone to the computer. Becoming computer literate, and learning the ins and outs of a word processor, can be trying at first. But after a brief time you will wonder how you ever wrote any other way. Revision is so much easier! You never have to retype a word that doesn't *need* retyping. Insertion of new material, cutting verbosity, and block operations such as moving a small piece of the story from page 2 to page 6, for example, all become a piece of cake. So if you don't have a small, good-quality computer, you might give the matter some serious thought.

*Don't,* however, use that kind of thinking as an excuse for any delay in moving ahead in the Map. There may be plenty of places where I remind you to slow down and do the work. But "spinning wool" or daydreaming about the computer in your future are not among the acceptable diversions or excuses.

If you can establish a regular work schedule specifying hours each day, so much the better for avoidance of daydreaming. If that's impossible, however, vow to set aside *some* time each day. Find a place where you will regularly work, too, whether it's a separate room converted to office space or a tiny corner of your bedroom.

Having a determination to work regularly and a place intended for that work often works wonders in itself. The growing writer is the writer who works virtually every day of the week, every week of the year.

Finally, you may notice that some of the earlier chapters are shorter than some that follow. There are two reasons for that: (1) You will be asked to do a considerable amount of unfamiliar preparatory work in the early chapters, and this must be taken one careful step at a time; and (2) as we progress into the territory outlined in the Map, we get into increasingly complex work—and increasing creativity on your part—that will require a bit more explanation and discussion in many cases.

## SUMMARY

The Map is a logical, step-by-step approach to the difficult, sometimes frustrating, always fascinating world of short fiction. A bedrock foundation of the system lies in the use of 3″ × 5″ or 4″ × 6″ filing cards, along with notebooks and colored pencils. You will be asked to start using some of these materials right away, so don't delay procuring them. You should also schedule times to work regularly, and find a regular place where that work will be done.

*Chapter Three*

# Taking Inventory of Yourself – and the Competition

---

PROGRESS CHECK:

✔ *Have you set a realistic schedule for work on a regular basis?*

✔ *Have you set up a workplace?*

✔ *Do you have your cards and other materials at hand?*

---

I'm fond of reminding student writers that they are not in a mere local competition; the competition they enter, when they set out to make a living as a writer, is global.

If any one of them wished to be successful as a doctor or as a salesperson, for example, they would "only" be required to outscore others in a med school class or outsell any other salesperson in Norman, Oklahoma. But the would-be writer must compete not only locally and regionally, and not even just nationally sometimes. The competition here is international.

Listen, some quiet night, when you've shirked your work that day because of fatigue or discouragement or distraction. Open a window of your house and listen attentively to the night sounds. Do you hear that distant, almost inaudible *clicking* sound? That's one of your competitors, pecking away at his keyboard, working away in the night in Paris or London or Erie, PA.

Now take your imagining a step further: Suppose the two of you are in similar stages of development as writers . . . and perhaps only one of you can make it.

Are you going to lose out because of procrastination or failure to put forth maximum effort?

Writing as a professional is not the easiest thing in the world. It demands the best of yourself and a clear understanding of what is desired in the commercial marketplace, where all your competitors are sending stories too.

If you are to succeed you must know, among other things, everything you can learn about yourself and the competition.

"But how can I learn more about myself?" you may ask. Let's look at that question first.

## TAKING INVENTORY OF YOURSELF

Unfortunately, daily living seldom leaves us much time for self-examination. Our usual educational methods stress rote learning or understanding of theories, not self-insight. As writers—whether beginning or pausing to take stock many years into a career—most of us need to take a self-inventory. Only in this way will we see ourselves clearly, be in close touch with our ideas, assumptions and emotions, and see the clearest and best path to our own inner creative wellsprings.

Emotion is crucial in good fiction. Therefore, it seems logical that the place to start on any self-evaluation should have to do with your feelings. Here then, is a procedure for delving into your own emotional makeup, the springs from which your most powerful fiction can flow.

On ten separate cards (you have the cards now, don't you?), write briefly about ten things or ideas or places or people or actions that you *feel very deeply about*. One card, one item.

A sentence may be enough in some cases, perhaps a word or two on others. (Example: "my faith in God." A somewhat less personal but equally good possibility: "the environment.")

A few of these cards may seem to write themselves because the subject is so much in your thoughts and feelings. But you may get stuck before you have ten cards filled out. If so, do three things for me: (1) Take your time; (2) don't give up; and (3) be honest with yourself.

There are potential pitfalls here. First, it might be easy to fill out some cards without much thought or self-examination. Be sure to ask yourself whether this is something you feel deeply about, or only believe you *should* feel deeply about. In addition, the deeply felt thing that leaps easily to mind should be examined more carefully. Ask yourself questions such as, "Why do I feel this deeply about this matter?" And, "Have my feelings on this changed over the years? How and why?"

Such additional thought can deepen your understanding of your own deepest emotions. You may wish to add observations to each card.

As to taking your time with this assignment, remember this: It might be easy to skip to the next point with only four or five cards filled out. But that would dilute the process of self-evaluation I'm trying to put you through here, and would cheat *you*. It would also start to set up a pattern of cheating on the entire procedure of the Map; so please take your time, and if you get discouraged, don't give up. Stick with it.

Be honest with yourself.

What is meant by that? Perhaps an example will explain. For years, in writing classes, I asked healthy, young students to write down on cards the ten things they felt most keenly about. I usually picked up the cards and examined them. There were many semesters when I picked up ten cards from each of twenty-five students in a class—250 cards!—and found that not a single one of them listed "love" or "romance" or "sex" among the top sources of feeling. The students had gone on automatic pilot and given me topics such as the environment, their grades, or the fate of the football team the following Saturday. Inadvertently they had not been honest with me—but, far more important, they had not been honest with themselves.

One is reminded of the would-be writer who carries a copy of a contemporary romance novel inside the dust jacket for a Charles Dickens classic to hide her true reading habits on the commuter train; then she does not write fiction of the type she enjoys and feels strongly about—romance—but instead frazzles her brains every night, trying to write about Dickensian situations, about which she really feels nothing.

This is why self-honesty is so important. Be truthful, and think and feel deeply here. No one is looking over your shoulder, and your future directions as a writer may come to be defined.

*You should stop reading here and do the assigned work before proceeding.*

♦ ♦ ♦

There. If you've followed instructions, you now have ten (or more) cards filled out with a few words on each. Put these aside for the time being; you'll want to come back to them later to reexamine their contents.

Now take another stack of cards. As time permits, fill them out in groups as follows.

- Five cards, each of which outlines or names a personal experience that aroused strong emotions in you.
- Five cards mentioning some idea or concept you deeply believe.
- Five cards listing an activity you very much like or enjoy.
- Five cards listing an activity you detest.
- Five places you like to go. (This may be a local movie theater, for example, or you might choose to name geographical sites such as the mountains of Colorado, perhaps, or the beach.)

Again, all these cards — like the first ten "feeling cards" — might be very brief. And again you will be well advised to write all of them before moving on.

◆ ◆ ◆

Finished? Good. If you've done the self-inventory work so far, we're beginning to make progress.

But we're not quite finished. The next few cards will require a bit more writing on them.

Here we go.

- On one card, write 35 to 75 words describing (in complete sentences) some event, specific activity or meeting that brought you great happiness sometime in the past.
- On another card, in the same number of words, describe an event, activity or meeting that brought you great sadness.
- On still another card, describe a time and place that made you very angry.
- And finally, describe a time and place that frightened you.

After completing these additional cards, find a file box of some kind (an old shoebox may do) where you can keep them. Devise category titles for them such as "Most Deeply Felt" and "Scariest." File away for now, but plan to take the cards out regularly to ponder them. Have you been honest with yourself in writing them? If you were to read these cards as if they had been written by someone else, what conclusions might you draw about the "kind of person" who wrote them?

In addition, plan to make this a continuing project. As other strong feelings surface, for example, or you find yourself reacting strongly to some person or event, fill out another card. Try to define as precisely as possible *what* aroused the feeling, what the feeling was, and how you might translate that event/feeling sequence into a bit of fiction.

Of such stuff is our self-understanding made. This insight is a continuing process of self-examination and discovery, and a search for ways to write about our deepest feelings in the most effective dramatic way.

Self-discovery is ongoing. We do not remain the same. Our feelings change, and so do our thoughts and activities. It is essential to be in contact with our feelings now, but it is equally important to continue to reevaluate ourselves to keep in touch with changes that may have taken place outside our full awareness. For only by being true to ourselves can we write at top form.

As time passes, you will find these cards provide a set of guidelines for the kinds of persons, places and things you should write about. That's because you have begun here to outline the sources of your most passionate feelings. And it is from these that the best fiction grows.

Does this imply autobiography? By no means. It simply recognizes the fact that we cannot write effective fiction about persons, things or situations we care little about.

So how have you been doing in your previous writing, perhaps before you were fully aware of the need to plumb your own deepest emotions? Look back now at some of your previous stories or fiction fragments. Have you been confronting the kinds of strong emotional material you just listed on some of your cards? *If not, why not?* Plan to change your methodology immediately.

It may be that you confront a feeling of personal joy or a deep commitment to the environment in the setting of a traditional western, for example. Or you may write from memory of a time in your life when you were extremely scared and angry—and do so in the framework of a romance. Good writers use their feelings, thoughts and memories in *whatever* kind of story they choose to write. In any story, the personal feeling will enrich the narrative.

If you find that you have indeed been writing from your personal storehouse of emotion, ask yourself if you could improve the copy in any way. Use some of your colored pencils in a system of your own devising to check your work for depth of feeling, and dramatic events likely to evoke those feelings.

For example, you might mark every direct statement of emotion — words such as "fear," "anger" or "sadness" in *red*. You might identify each segment of the story designed to evoke a strong feeling, bracket it in, say, *green*, then write the specific intended feeling in the margin. If you find a character showing feeling, you might underline that segment in *blue*, and so on.

Having done this emotion inventory of your copy, ask yourself if you could sharpen anything to make it more heartfelt. If you find changes to make, go ahead and make them.

Finally, having done the revision, stand back and examine what you have done to see if there is any *pattern* in it. Perhaps, for example, all the changes you just made were to add emotion . . . take a certain aloofness or chill tone out of the story. Or perhaps you noticed characters seeming too histrionic about something you don't really care that much about.

Awareness of any such tendencies, seen more clearly after some self-inventory — when the copy was "cold" — can help you write more emotionally, more honestly, and more deeply the next time you start a story.

In the last three chapters of this book we will return to self-evaluation in terms of your copy, and provide additional elements you eventually will look for in writing and revising. For now, however, concern about your *general* tendencies, as you see them, will furnish a starting point.

Whatever observations you make about your own work, as it relates to feeling, should be written down in some form. Ideally, this is where you will make an entry in one of your notebooks, one you can label "journal." You may already have such a volume. If so, fine. If not, start one now. Take the time to write down an observation about your own work tendencies, because you might forget it and make the same mistake over again.

Please take as much time as needed to do the work suggested so far in this chapter.

## TAKING INVENTORY OF THE COMPETITION

Learning all you can about the competition is also very important to you as a writer expanding her horizons. The procedure is not as personally harrowing as the self-inventory sometimes turns out to be, but it also is a multistep process. Again we will use cards.

Identify some current publications that carry fiction of the kind you would like to write. Then, for each publication, fill in a group of cards containing the following information.

Note the usual length of stories. Take the time to count words in several stories. If you find a great variety of lengths, check another issue or two; the one you first checked may not be typical. Most publications have a "favored length," and publish shorter material only as necessary to "fill." Some may buy three stories of 3,000 words each per month, but only one story of 6,000. Obviously with such a publication you will stand a chance three times better with a 3,000-word story than with one of 6,000 words. Such a simple observation, duly noted on a card, can help you.

Note, please, that I'm not suggesting you should always wrench your short story into some perceived market trend or peculiarity. But sometimes adapting your story length to 3,000 words, for example, might involve a matter as simple as taking out a minor subplot or eliminating one interesting—but not vital—character. When such simple changes can be made without harm to the basic story, why not make them to give the story a better chance of seeing the light of day in a given magazine?

Note, too, the usual kind of subject matter in your study publication. This may be hard to identify. Try your best.

• The usual type of setting. Characteristically a magazine will publish most of its stories with a particular kind of setting: large city, urban slum, rural countryside, whatever. Identifying this preference again can help you.

• The usual kind of characters. Is there a detectable pattern in age? Sex? Economic standing? Appearance? Job or housing?

• The usual mode of narration. Confession-type stories are almost all first-person. Does your study magazine also like first-person narration, or does it tend to publish third-person?

• The usual language style. Is the language simple, even down-home? Or elaborate and even convoluted? Editors' preferences for style can make or break a submission. If the apparent style seems far different from your own, you might be well advised to look for another market, rather than trying to write in a style that doesn't come naturally to you.

• The usual method of opening and closing the story. Does the story usually begin "in medias res" — in the middle of things, such as dialogue or action, or does it begin at a more leisurely pace? Does the opening tend to identify a person (central character) and personal problem at once, or later? Does the opening segment of a few paragraphs depend mainly on content or style or mood to draw the reader in? Do the stories generally end well or badly for the characters? Are the endings sad or happy, or ambiguous?

Other questions to ask about a publication may occur to you. Fill out cards for them, too, as they occur. When you come upon a published story that you particularly like, study it from every angle you can think of, including those listed in a general way above. Ask yourself additional questions about the time span of the story, its setting and the mood it evokes. Do you want to write like this? How is it done? Fill out as many additional observation cards as you can think of. Plan to keep them, too, as part of your growing inventory of facts about yourself and the competition.

As with your feeling cards, you should devise category titles for any observation cards you fill out: perhaps such titles as "length," "typical setting" or "number of characters." Of course you will think of more categories — and more meaningful ones — than these. The key here, again, is to record observed information so it will not be forgotten or lost.

These categories will be useful to you for years. Such analysis of self and markets as briefly outlined here should become a habit of a lifetime. Such cards should be added to . . . changed or deleted . . . throughout your working life. For they represent things a writer must always be aware of . . . must always reexamine on a regular basis.

## SUMMARY

In this chapter I have worked to convince you that you can write your most effective short (or long) fiction only if you base it on strong feelings you have experienced. But before you can do this, you must take inventory of yourself emotionally to be sure what your strongest feelings are, and where the sources of these feelings lie. And you must be rigorously honest with yourself!

Vital, too, is constant reevaluation of your own copy, checking it for maximum effectiveness from every angle you can think of at this stage in your development.

To do your best, you must also inventory the competition out there, and work to devise methods by which you can learn from that competition in published markets.

As a system for accomplishing these goals, you should use filing cards, thus establishing a lifetime work-habit that will benefit you in many more ways, as shall become evident as you proceed through the Map.

And one more word about slowing down and being patient. In the few pages of this chapter you have been asked to do an incredible amount of work. Some of it is based on principles we haven't fully discussed yet, and some of it may be personally trying for you. *Take your time.* We aren't in a race here.

Only when you feel finished with the minimum suggested work should you move on to chapter four.

*Chapter Four*

# Beginning to Select Your Characters

PROGRESS CHECK:

✔ *Have you begun an extensive collection of cards in all the categories listed in chapter three?*

✔ *Have you begun or added to your journal?*

✔ *Have you analyzed published copy as well as some of your own?*

S ome writers begin imagining a new story by thinking of a place, while others might begin with thoughts about a theme, or about plot events, or about a particular scene. But even if they start with one of these fiction bases, it is seldom long before they also begin to think about the people who will carry out the action of the story.

To speak of a piece of fiction without people in it is virtually a contradiction in terms. That's because stories exist to tell about people — their activities, their thoughts and their feelings.

Effective stories are about people. Even those rare tales that feature animals or other nonhuman creatures succeed only insofar as they can build their "characters" on human characteristics. From the tales of Beatrix Potter to Tolkien's Hobbit, stories that don't have people at their heart use peoplelike creatures with human ideas, attitudes, feelings and actions to help the reader identify with them . . . to convince the reader that he should *care* about them.

So, while your next step in creating more building blocks for your story might have to do with setting or plot structure, it seems more logical to look next at your story characters, and how you can begin a process of self-examination and imagining designed to put the most vivid and interesting characters into that next story.

Story characters are much more than names and brief descriptions. You the writer must bring them to life. You must have convincing, lifelike people at the very center of your stories. That means you need vivid story characters, ones the reader will identify with, and love—or hate.

Learning how to create vivid characters and fit them into your stories is a lifelong challenge, but you can start here and now. The basis of a technique that will help you may seem so simple on its surface you may not immediately trust it. But if you give it a chance, it will help you greatly in discovering the kinds of characters you will want in your stories—and how best to show the kind of people they are. It will also give you a methodology for advancing your craftsmanship through *work*, not daydreaming.

As before, we'll use cards. On the first fresh, blank card in front of you, describe very briefly a single aspect of personality that you find appealing. Very often this can be a single word. But just as often you may make your desirable aspect of personality more specific by adding a word or two.

For example, you might list on the top of Card No. 1 the word *kindness*. All well and good. But you might want to narrow this broad description by adding a few more words, such as in the following examples:

- Kindness—to people with problems in their lives.
- Kindness—to helpless animals and the sick.
- Kindness—even to nasty people causing trouble in your life.
- Kindness—to children.

A word of warning: Be alert to the danger of defining one desirable trait with the name of another. For example, if you wrote "Kindness—by being generous with money to the poor," then maybe you haven't qualified your definition of "kindness" so much as you've identified a second nice trait that ought to head a card of its own—*generosity*.

By filling out your cards in this way, you not only begin to define for yourself what *your* central definition of "kindness" (or whatever) is all about; you also begin to crystallize the kinds of kindness you might soon want to show in a character in a story.

You may find that you can't narrow your definition of kindness quite this specifically. Do your best; if you think kindness is a most desirable aspect of personality, you must have *some* set of attitudes in mind when you use the word. The addition of qualifiers behind the general trait may be a struggle for you, but it's a useful focusing device.

An added word of caution: Just as important as adding qualifiers is resistance to the temptation to *write too much*. If you find yourself wanting to add a great deal of qualifiers behind the general word or phrase, you may be failing to sufficiently define the personality traits in the first place. At this step in defining character traits, you are seeking to *isolate* and *narrowly define* each trait you put on a card. The suggestion that you add a word or two to the general descriptor is not so that you can broaden your definition; quite to the contrary, I'm asking you to sharpen your definition with such a qualifier.

Narrow one aspect of kindness, and put only that on the card in front of you. Make sure you don't write more than a line or two. Going beyond that might get you into the morass of filling out card after card, providing an encyclopedic definition. That's not what we're after here. Specify in a few words, and get on. If another aspect of kindness, for example, cries out for expression, fill out a second card.

Please note, however, that no one is going to force you to write more than a single word atop a card right now. You may qualify the word slightly if you wish, but it isn't absolutely necessary at this point.

Far more important than honing a precise definition for the general trait is identifying it. And more important than identifying one such trait that you find desirable is the identification of many you may like. You can't plan to spend a career building every likeable character on the same nice aspect of personality.

So, as soon as you have one card filled out with a word (or six), I want you to fill out at least nineteen more cards that list personality aspects you personally find appealing or sympathetic or good. I hope these twenty total cards will identify at least fifteen *different* desirable traits (allowing for more than one card in a few cases).

This process may take more than a few minutes but should not be an onerous task. Take the time to fill out these cards now, before proceeding.

◆ ◆ ◆

Now that you've finished, let's take another step in search of character values.

Having identified admirable personality traits, you have taken an important step in beginning to identify the kind of person you will likely put at the center of your story. But it usually takes more than one person to make a story, and very often the character second in importance in a story is in conflict with the first. So as soon as you've filled out your first twenty character cards, you need to start identifying traits you can give to the second person in the story — the one who very often will cause trouble for your Mr. or Ms. Nice Guy — the character many call "the villain."

Thus we come to Job No. 2: Fill out another twenty cards, each of which identifies some aspect of personality you find ugly or despicable. Try to be very brief and specific, just as before. Again, remember you're trying to isolate a trait on each card here, not provide an in-depth definition of one.

You may find that your "bad-guy cards" often turn out to be the flip side of the desirable trait cards. That's probably to some degree inevitable. If you put "generosity" on one desirable trait card, chances are that one of your twenty undesirable cards will list a word like "stinginess or "selfishness." No problem with that. But if you find some descriptors turning up on one list and not on the other, that's OK too. This is not a test. It's more an inventory of yourself and the kind of people you will want in your stories.

It's also important to realize that these cards don't have to be consistent with one another. If some of your cards assume a female person, and others a male, there's no problem. You'll mix and match characters much later. Also, if you realize that a few cards make you think of a real person in your life, while another card may have popped into mind along with some favorite character you met in reading fiction, that's OK too. Where the ideas and ideals come from is of no consequence at this point. To make the point once more: We're building a stockpile of cards listing generally abstract personality characteristics we like and dislike; nothing more.

Again, it may take a while to fill out these additional cards. Do it now, before proceeding. If impatience gnaws at you, remember this: These cards will also be going into your filing box, and they will be a basis for many characters in many future stories. They are the bedrock of your "story people inventory," and well worth the effort.

## ADDING TAGS TO ILLUSTRATE TRAITS

If you stop to think about it for a moment, you'll realize that in real life we usually judge a person by how he looks, speaks and acts, rather than by what some other acquaintance may tell us about him.

"You'll like Joe," a friend tells you. "Everyone likes him immediately—he's so amusing and witty and friendly to everyone."

Now, you might have the words "witty," "amusing" and "friendly" atop three of your desirable personality trait cards. But chances are that you won't be convinced about Joe just because someone describes him this way. Chances are about fifty-fifty, as a matter of fact, that you'll meet Joe with an attitude of "OK, big guy, prove to me just how witty and wonderful you are, because I don't believe it for a minute!"

It's the same in writing your short story. It's all well and good for you to know now that a desirable aspect of personality, for you, is kindness. But if you just tell your reader, "Milly was a kind person," your reader isn't going to believe it for a second.

Why? Because description of a trait—what you have on your cards so far—is *abstract*. And in fiction, as in real life, we judge people not by abstractions but by observing them and then drawing conclusions.

Which means—oh my, a complication here in characterizing story people—we can't just say they're kind, or whatever. We have to devise ways to *prove it to the reader*.

Well, that may not be as hard as it sounds. We've got traits already identified. They tend to be abstract and internal—inside the character. So all we have to do is figure a way to translate the abstract-internal into the concrete-external.

How do we do that? By devising a tag (or two) to show every trait.

The tag is an appearance, an action, a mannerism, a habit of speech, or other outward, physical, simple, concrete thing about the character that your reader can visualize or imagine hearing, or understand with the senses in some way. So a character you identify as selfish and miserly might, as one of his tags, refuse to let his suffering young clerk put enough coal on the office stove; he might rub his fingers together in the classic stage action of the greedy miser; and he might even have a name that somehow *sounds* miserly and miserable—Ebenezer Scrooge.

To put all this another way, your job as a writer intent on building memorable characters is twofold: First you identify strong traits, admirable or despicable. Then you devise character tags you can hang on your character to illustrate the abstract trait.

So your character Milly, earlier described as "kind," should have one or more concrete tags to *prove* she has the trait of kindness. What might these tags be? Perhaps she drives a "meals-on-wheels" van to take food to the housebound even though the job pays nothing. Perhaps she has the habit of smiling even when her hateful sister attacks her verbally. Perhaps she has the habit of saying that it's possible to find good qualities in anyone.

Or perhaps you can come up with much better simple tags — of action, appearance and speech, in the examples I just provided — to show the abstract quality of kindness. Take a minute or two here and grab any one of the trait cards you filled out earlier. There will be plenty of blank space left on it. Write down the briefest possible notation of one, two or three specific, concrete tags you might use to illustrate — and prove to your doubting reader — that Milly really does have kindness in her heart, or whatever.

I imagine that you came up with far better tags than the ones I listed for you. If you had any trouble, however, be of good cheer: This is an area of writing that becomes easier with practice.

The one other thing we need to remember about character tags at this point is that the tag *must be repeated often* to be sure the reader notices it. Thus Milly wouldn't merely be seen driving her meals-on-wheels van just once. This tag for her kindness would be displayed often, and perhaps in other ways. She might also be seen talking on the telephone to some volunteer supervisor and saying she put her own money into fuel for the van that day, rather than run late; she might have the van parked in her driveway, and we might see it there once; she might have a little backache from wheeling the van around in traffic.

A tag is too precious to mention once and forget. And readers are too inattentive to catch on if you wave a tag just once. You must plan to wave your tags often.

Before moving beyond this chapter, your next assignment is to do for all your trait cards what you were asked to do for one: that is, devise one or more tags to illustrate the listed trait.

In many cases these will be tags of action, like Milly driving the van. Others might be tags of mannerism, such as the greedy man habitually rubbing his hands together in anticipation of money. Others might be tags of speech, such as a character who might repeat several times in a story some word or phrase such as, "I don't know why everyone is against me!" In a few instances, you might have tags of general appearance, such as the story bully's thick, brutally powerful hands and forearms.

Take your time and think about the various kinds of tags *you* might use for your growing characters on the trait cards. Remember that this work is probably going to go directly into one of your stories in the near future. So again, take your time.

This is a far bigger and more creative task than any you've been assigned yet here in the Map. You'll need to have this work done shortly, however, to move on to the next step of creating your story.

Look for the most vivid and convincing tag you can locate for each trait. Remember that the best tag is not a whole subplot of events or even a long paragraph, but something short that can be shown several times, perhaps in different ways, during the course of your story. You want things like little quirky habits, favorite words or phrases in speech, or an attitude, perhaps, that can be repeated over and over. (So if you had a little girl with the abstract trait of *vanity*, perhaps you would—like Charles Schulz in "Peanuts" — have her constantly pat her head, and pose, and talk about how lucky she is to have naturally curly hair.)

If you find that you have written down one tag, and then later think of a better one for that trait, don't hesitate to go back and change the card.

## THE VALUE OF EXAGGERATION

If you happen to find yourself devising some pretty outlandish tags, I hope you will *not* automatically censor such ideas. While all tags can't be wildly imaginative, it's a fact of fiction-writing life that the best and most memorable characters very often are wildly exaggerated in terms of both traits and tags.

Thus a character will not be merely selfless and loyal to his combat unit buddies, for example; he will be *extremely* selfless and loyal. And as a tag he will not merely tell his buddies they're nice guys. He'll consistently volunteer for dangerous patrols, to save them the danger; he may give up his own chance for rotation back to safety because he believes a pal deserves it more; he won't mention just once that his first loyalty is to his buddies—he'll say it, he'll write it in a letter home, he'll think about it a lot, and he'll constantly worry about his pals' safety.

Such a character of extremes, exaggerated in terms of tags, might seem too obvious to you at this point as you devise your tag cards.

But please believe me: Readers of fiction—especially of the short story—need strong exaggeration to make it possible for them to visualize the character at all. You may have to tone down some tags later, but at this point let your imagination run free. These cards are not final copy; they're working cards, and other steps will be taken with them.

To put it another way: Better exaggeration than meekness at this point in the creative process, particularly in short fiction where you don't have much space. You can always go back and "tame things down" a bit, if your later reflection indicates that a particular tag or series of tags really did become too exaggerated or wild. On the other hand, it's often almost impossible to strengthen a character's tags late in the story-revision process, because he or she has already come into fictional existence as gray and even dull.

You can have fun with this assignment. You can at the same time build a gold mine of material for your story people.

## SUMMARY

People are what make your story. The more believable and vivid they are, the better your story is likely to be.

Your first step in building credible characters is to identify personality traits that you find likeable or positive in the people around you. You need a stockpile of these traits, on cards. You will also benefit from having a collection of cards that identify negative characters—ones you would not like in real life, and can make unlikeable in your fiction. Use of these traits will give force to your stories because they come out of your own unique preferences and perceptions about people—and life.

Traits are abstract, and readers need proof—things that are concrete, specific and credible. To provide concreteness for traits, which tend to hide inside the character, the writer must devise tags—outward, physical details the reader can see and hear that demonstrate the trait inside.

There is no sin in exaggeration when it comes to fiction characters.

Creation of trait and tag cards is not something you should do quickly, just for this chapter, and then forget. This card collection should be added to regularly, as long as you get new ideas or meet new and interesting people who fire your imagination.

# THE ARCHITECTURE
# OF STORY

As you've already noted, most of the material you'll find in this book calls on you to perform specific tasks, usually with filing cards, to build your plan for your own story. As mentioned in chapter one, however, there are some other aspects of short story writing that don't lend themselves exactly to the task-oriented approach. We're talking about generalized concepts, attitudes about fiction, or mental models concerning fiction that most successful writers carry around in their heads and seldom (if ever) specify for anyone else.

In academia, they would call these generalizations "syntheses," or "paradigms." They reflect broad views and insights into fiction, and how it works, which you'll ultimately understand fully only after working through the regular chapters of this book and then forming your own conclusions about how fiction "works" for you.

But just because you'll ultimately come to your own synthesis is no reason not to take time out from card-work now and then to look at the "big picture." We'll do this in sections such as this one, interspersed among the work chapters.

This is the first such Time Out, of course, and it's fitting that we first try to get a panoramic view of what the architecture of "story" usually involves.

Now, if you have been reading much current short fiction, you may be astounded to hear someone suggest that any architecture exists in much of what is published today. Superficially, it would appear that while longer fiction has become more and more structured in ways we can analyze, published short fiction is becoming more unpredictable and eccentric—with no obvious rhyme or reason—all the time.

On the surface, yes, that is true. In commercial long fiction (novels) we have such categories as the classic mystery, the romance, the western, the "techno-thriller," and the historical, each of which has identifying characteristics. Further, in the contemporary novel, you can easily identify at least some aspects of an architecture, such as that almost all novels are divided into chapters.

Short stories today would appear on first examination not to have anything in common. You find short-shorts (mood pieces of only a few hundred words) and long "short" stories (those that fall below the usual stated minimum of 60,000 words for a novel, but run far beyond the norms of something in the neighborhood of 3,000 to 5,000 for a conventional short story). You find all kinds of viewpoint structure, all kinds of authorial voices, and all kinds of problems—or lack of same.

Under the seeming chaos of contemporary short fiction, however, you can still detect basic assumptions about story architecture that *generally* apply. Note that I said "generally." There is an exception to every rule. But sometimes we can see patterns if we step back far enough and don't get tangled up in the details.

If you were asked to define the architecture of a "shelter," for example, you might look at a Cape Cod home, an old midwestern farmhouse, a Chicago apartment building, a southwestern ranch, an adobe home in a place like Santa Fe, a log cabin in Utah and an igloo in Alaska, and throw up your hands declaring that these shelters had nothing in common.

If you looked from a broader perspective, however, you could come up with an "architecture of shelter." It would include such aspects as *walls* and a *roof* of some kind. There would usually be a way to get into and out of the place, a door or portal or perhaps even a hole in the roof with a ladder. There would be a way to look outside (probably), and some kind of flooring. You would usually find a chimney or hole or something to let out cooking and heating odors and smoke. I leave you to think a bit further about such very generalized aspects of "shelter."

Devising such a broad definition of "shelter," designed to cover a multitude of variations, seems simple enough. But if you were to allow yourself to notice whether the walls were brick or wood or adobe or stone or ice, then you could quickly get into trouble and figure there was no commonality.

That's often what we do with the short story when we begin to think there is no broadly defining architecture.

So then what *are* some of these elements that tend to occur in almost all short stories, however different their bricks and mortar might be? Let's look at some of the parts of broad story architecture. But please remember: We're looking for *generalizations* here, ones that might even occasionally be violated by some story that falls outside all predictable norms. (To put it another way, we're looking for principles that will provide insight into what a Cape Cod home might have in common with a thatched-roof hut in Guatemala.) Might an architect benefit from having such a paradigm in his mind when he starts to design his next house? I think so. Similarly, having such a wide paradigm for the short story will give you a vast blueprint into which you can fit your story-writing techniques and puzzle pieces.

## COMMON STORY ELEMENTS

First, a short story is *longer than a vignette, but shorter than a novelette*. This may sound absurdly simple, but some useful further distinctions can be drawn from even this truism.

In the mind of most writers, a piece of work becomes a *story* when it goes beyond the few hundred words usually defining a vignette. And what is a vignette? It is a picture. It is a static photograph. It looks at a frozen point in time and space, and tries to get at that moment's essence. It does not move and it does not necessarily even deal with people.

The writer's purpose in producing a vignette is not to tell any kind of tale so much as it is to crystallize a place or event or time, and somehow evoke the desired feeling in the reader. Above all else, it stands still. There is no space for more than one evocative description or statement. Indeed, there is no desire on the part of the writer to produce more than that.

The reader of a vignette, meanwhile, is not looking for narrative or development of events. She is looking for a moment's escape from the everyday, a quick and usually simple single emotion or impression—the kind of result one gets from a poem by Emily Dickenson.

A short story, on the other hand, is longer than a vignette. It cannot be sustained on mere tone or mood alone, and the writer does not desire to try. There is space enough to tell a tale, and both the writer and the reader want more than merely to know a static instant; they want to develop a moving event or series of events that arouses curiosity about "how things are going to turn out." This might be accomplished in 3,000 words or perhaps even less, but ordinarily not more than 5,000—or, rarely, maybe 7,500.

The short story is longer than a vignette, then, but is not the vast canvas of the novel or even the novelette. The allowance for additional words gives the writer space enough for some development. On the other hand, however, there are practical length limits which normally reduce the cast of characters and the amount of time that can be covered.

These limitations are at once the weakness and the power of every successful short story. The writer has recognized the limits, in both directions, and has done what should be done in a short story, but has not fallen into the disaster of trying to tell too much—more than the fragile form can deliver in limited words.

The wise short story writer, then, will plan enough material to allow for development, but will ruthlessly avoid the trap of hoping to cram too much into a small box.

Is it too obvious to say that the short story, ninety-nine times out of a hundred, is *written down*? I think not. All of us like to tell stories from time to time, but all of us are not short story writers. To qualify as a short story, the tale must be committed to paper in a language others can understand. "Putting it down" is often hard work, which weeds out the would-be short story writers who only make up things orally at camp or on the front porch.

This is not to disparage oral storytellers or historians or others who perhaps visit the library and spin yarns to the delight of wide-eyed youngsters. Such storytelling is a gift. But the point to be made here is that a narrower definition is required if we are to fit our work into a general theoretical blueprint. Otherwise we might end up talking our stories away, or carrying them to the local club meeting where our acting ability could become more important than the tale itself—the dramatic style of delivery hiding all sorts of possible deficiencies in the story itself.

The lesson is simple enough. A short story is written down; therefore, if you want to create short stories, you have to go through the process of putting them on paper. Let everyone else talk about stories. *You* write them!

Another aspect of short story architecture is that *there is a viewpoint*. Now, while viewpoint as a technique is treated elsewhere in the Map, here the point is simply that short stories, like most longer forms, are characterized by giving the reader a way to experience the action of the story as seen through the eyes of some character inside the action.

This is remarkable in itself. Probably the first short stories were autobiographical: A traveler went off on a journey, perhaps, and had an adventure; when he came back home, he recited the events to the others around the campfire. But soon the listeners or readers became more sophisticated, and the would-be short-storyteller or writer could not go out every day and have some new true adventure. And so he hit upon the idea of *making up* a story, and getting the listeners involved by helping them pretend that *they* were in the story action — thus providing the reader identification that is created in every short story using the technique of viewpoint.

The lesson to be drawn from this generalization is that you should always know who your viewpoint character is, and you should stick with that viewpoint character throughout if you can. For we all live our lives in a single viewpoint — our own — and we most readily accept the credibility of stories we are told if we can identify with someone experiencing that story from inside, from a viewpoint as limited as our own in real life.

Movies, of course, seldom if ever have a real viewpoint of the type we're discussing here. Movies have camera angles. That's why some truly fine movie writers have failed as short story or novel writers. They freewheel all over the landscape in telling the story, and the reader can never believe any of it, and never knows exactly where he is supposed to be standing in order to orient himself. In a good short story, the writer is inside the story itself, and brings the reader in with her.

Another crucial aspect of the short story is that it has *movement*. Ways of attaining that movement are discussed elsewhere in the Map. Here it's sufficient to point out that such movement is part of the short story paradigm.

Most readers simply can't be held for 3,000 or more words if the situation on the page is completely static. Such static "storytelling" is boring, among other things. So the short story starts somewhere and some time, and ends up somewhere and some time else. The movement may be extremely subtle, but there is movement.

As a writer, you can't simply sit around in your story and endlessly describe a frozen tableau. A major part of your job is to figure out where and when the story starts, and where and when it ends, and *what it means to someone* (the viewpoint character of the story).

There is more here than meets the eye. What I am suggesting is that you might have physical action taking place in your story, but that does not in itself mean that *anything is happening*. For something to "happen," there has to be impact on some person in the story. If things take place but don't mean anything, they're like that riddle tree that falls when no one is around. Who really cares if there's a sound when the tree falls in a deserted forest? What difference does it make to anyone? The crash is significant only if it makes someone jump.

What does all this mean to you? It means you must contrive tales that move, and move in ways that affect story people, changing them—their actions, their insights, their feelings—something. It means you cannot stand around, page after page, and try out different stylistic tricks to describe the same stuff over and over. It *may* mean that, while a short story often is done in a beautiful writing style, you might easily get hung up on style to the detriment of providing movement. It *could* even mean that far too many writers worry about style when they ought to be getting off their narrative duff and getting the story under way.

Another architectural feature that short stories have is *dynamic emotion*. By this I mean that the short story almost always deals with deeply felt emotions inside the characters. This emotion is seldom the same at the end of the story as it was at the beginning. In this regard, virtually every successful short story is in some way a *Pilgrim's Progress*, the story of a person involved in a quest, and who is changed in the pursuit. Thus, every good writer's definition of the short story includes moving story people emotionally—dealing with personal issues.

This does not necessarily mean what is usually termed "emotional writing." Your style may help you deal with story feelings in an intense and subjective manner, getting deep inside one character.

On the other hand, your style may *appear to be* rather objective even though the story deals with powerful emotions that are shown in ways other than character introspection. The classic example of this approach is the work of Ernest Hemingway, in which what looks like objective reportage is actually the recording of highly selected impressions that tell the reader with stark clarity what the characters are experiencing emotionally.

Whatever your selected approach or style, in other words, you must come to grips with strong emotions in your stories. This means that you must imagine your characters' feelings most intensely, which can be an exhausting and harrowing experience when you are writing your very best. The short story does not leave room for emotional cowards. The portrayal of powerful emotions — however accomplished, even in the seemingly quietest story — is part of short story architecture.

Another aspect of the modern short story's architecture is that it is told through *narration, description, internalization* and *action* — any one of these, but usually in a felicitous blending of all of them. It's necessary to understand how each of these aspects contributes to the umbrella definition of "short story" we're working on here.

## NARRATION

Narration is sometimes loosely defined to include oral storytelling (which we've already eliminated from our specialized definition), detailed telling of events which might include imagined conversation, and even moment-by-moment action. In our fine-tuned definition, however, we mean the author's telling of a flow of events in the swiftest, most condensed possible form.

For example, let's suppose that two people start on a car trip together. They encounter heavy rain near Indianapolis, pass a serious car wreck in St. Louis, and stop for the night in Rolla, Missouri. Assuming that the rain, the wreck and the selection of a motel in Rolla are significant developments, an author might choose to give several pages to details about this trip, including talk between the characters, struggling against the blinding rain, and stopping to see if they could help at the scene of the wreck. This *might* be done, but chances are that in a short story, with its demand for condensation, the whole trip would be put in narration, like this:

They left Columbus at 6:15 A.M. and ran into rain near Indianapolis. It was tough going. They saw a serious wreck in St. Louis, then bedded down for the night in Rolla, Missouri.

This is narration: a condensed record of events, told by the author as swiftly and concisely as possible to get a record into the story.

Narration obviously speeds the story along, and allows the writer to include a number of events that short story length limitations might not allow to be included in more detailed form. This is all to the good. The bad part about narration, on the other hand, is that it is not as involving or exciting for the reader as more detailed presentation might be. Take a minute or two right here, for example, and think about how you might present the trip in a series of dramatic, detailed episodes; there could be arguments between the characters in the car, even disagreement before they leave about the wisdom of making the trip at all with bad weather to the west. Then each new setback along the way could intensify the basic argument, leading to bitterness between the characters, and so on.

Take a moment to think about this, imagining other ways to develop the material.

◆ ◆ ◆

Your few moments of thought undoubtedly showed you that writers sacrifice drama and reader involvement by dropping into narration. But narration *is* a part of most stories' architecture. The key for you is to know when you can or should use it, and when an event is too important to summarize in the form of narration.

## DESCRIPTION

Description, as you know, is also a part of short story architecture. It's vital to keep the reader physically grounded in the story world. Whether you are telling the reader how a street or business office looks, or telling him what a character looks like, your job is to appeal to the senses—sight usually being the most important sense—to help him visualize places and people. Virtually all short stories contain an element of description.

The problem with stopping to describe something or someone is that more often than not you *do* stop to do it. What does this mean? Simply that forward movement of events—a crucial element of storytelling—halts while you describe. Too much description can stop a story dead in its tracks, never to get going again.

What this implies for you the writer is twofold:

• Description must be as brief and as evocative as possible, within the severe word limits of a short story.

• Description "on the run" (while movement is taking place) should be used whenever possible.

On the first of these two points, a writer often begins a writing career because her talent first showed in writing description. School-teachers at the elementary level dearly love to give writing assignments asking each student to describe a trip or a beautiful scene or a loved one. There is certainly nothing wrong with this; it teaches observation and the careful selection of words that will best describe something.

This presents two potential problems, however. First, such assignments are seldom if ever made in the context of brevity or condensation. Often the reverse is true, and the longest paper gets the best grade. This tends to engrain wordy habits that can kill a short story. Second, the writer who got wonderful comments from the teacher on lengthy descriptions probably considers this a strong point in her style, and loves to drop such passages into her stories, often to the detriment of progress of the tale.

The implication of all this is straightforward enough: The more you like to write static description, the more you will have to be alert to the danger of verbosity—and slash your descriptions as sharply as possible while using strong evocative nouns and verbs to stand for much longer strings of adjectives and adverbs. (If you have a passage that takes 200 words to tell how dynamically and energetically Pauline enters a room, you may want to cut *all* the adjectives and adverbs and simply write, "Pauline exploded into the room.")

In a similar fashion, necessary description is made less dangerous to story pacing if you can slip it in during character movement. Have your character walk to work, and while on the way *notice* the old clock tower, the morning fog, and the deepening chill rather than giving the reader a static author-objective description. It's also far more effective to have your character pick up bits and pieces of descripion of another character—her facial expression, hair and clothing, for example—during a stressful or interesting conversation, rather than lecturing the reader in a static manner about what the new character is like. Readers won't as likely be hung up by description, in other words, if it's given as part of ongoing development.

## INTERNALIZATION

Internalization is another characteristic of short story architecture that deserves thought and attention on the writer's part. This aspect of architecture involves what's going on inside the character from whose viewpoint the story is being told. It includes emotions and thoughts.

Now, some stories are very thin on internalization, and others are packed with it. In terms of your awareness of the technique, the provisos are similar to those concerning description. Internalization is good stuff, and keeps the reader strongly connected to the character, understanding his problems and how he may be suffering.

There is a universalizing effect to be gained from emotional internalization in a short story: We all experience the same gamut of feelings at one time or another, and when the writer shows some of these feelings through internalization in a story, the reader tends to "connect" emotionally with the character as well as with the issues at hand in the story.

There is a logical effect to be gained from thought-internalization in a story. When the reader sees how the character is thinking and planning his next story move, the reader is much more likely to understand why things are happening as they are—and much more likely to believe the story. Thus internalization can bring both emotional contact with the character (sympathy) and understanding of motivation (logic and credibility) to the story.

But, as with description, when you pause to tell how the character is feeling or thinking, the story's movement stops. And so, as powerful as internalization can be, the wise writer is wary of extended passages of pure internal analysis of the character. In its place, and in proportion, it's wonderful; carried to an extreme, it can bring the story to a dead halt, killing reader interest in a story person who simply seems to *sit* there, feeling and thinking.

Also, too much internalization can kill story tension since the writer explains away everything, denying the reader the pleasure of making his own discoveries. It's the old admonition that the writer of fiction must show, not tell.

How much internalization will you have in your story? It depends on your perceived strengths as a writer, the kind of story you intend to tell, and the kind of character you plan to deal with. In a quiet story of discovery about a young woman suffering depression, great gobs of the telling might involve silent, unmoving meditation in a rocker beside a frozen bedroom window. In a story of conflict, on the other hand, a vastly different kind of character will be involved, and you might have almost no internalization.

Elsewhere in this book, you can find further discussion of this question, as well as of others touched on in this Time Out. Here the intent is not to offer practical work concerning the technique or idea, but to put the concept into some kind of larger perspective. So you can be sure you will hear more about these matters in the context of specific assignments.

## ACTION

Action, the final characteristic of this category, really consists of three different kinds of story-presentation: dialogue, maneuver and transition. All of these are treated elsewhere in the context of how you plan them and use them in your story. But a brief overview here may help.

Dialogue, of course, is talking by story characters. Most short stories today have it as an ingredient; the day of the first-person narrator, talking narrative to the reader as if he were in the same room with him, is pretty well over. Readers get involved when story people talk to one another. Dialogue is a key way of showing conflict between people, and of characterizing them through what they say and how they say it.

Dialogue, however, is *not* story people talking *at* one another. There is a vast difference between speech-making and give-and-take dialogue. Real people interrupt one another, ramble, may repeat key words, and may get into question and answer. They may be verbose.

Dialogue in a story, however, is usually characterized by—here's that word again—brevity. And by condensation. Dialogue in a story is *not* often truly realistic. It merely looks realistic because it is finely honed, trimmed as sharply as possible, and then honed again by the writer.

Maneuver is an ingredient of most modern short stories. By "maneuver," I simply mean that most short stories today involve at least two people somehow at odds with one another—trying to get the same thing, or trying to understand one another, or perhaps trying to deceive one another. The primary characters circle and spar, trying this and then that, moving as if in a boxing match or a fencing exhibition. Maneuver in your story may be violent or it may be exceedingly quiet and subtle. At some level, however, it ought to be there. Short story architecture is exceedingly broad, but character maneuver is almost always an element.

You need to remain aware of one point made earlier in this Time Out: Movement is vital. One of the best ways to provide movement is by keeping the major characters in touch with each other, and involved in some variety of maneuver. (If you follow instructions for plot and character development as given elsewhere in this book, incidentally, you will almost certainly achieve maneuver. But often it helps to see how a piece of the puzzle fits into a general definition.)

Finally, another kind of action involves *transition*. This word describes passages that get a character from one place to another, or from one time to another. In all modern short stories, transition is made as brief as possible.

Many writers worry excessively about handling transition. "How do I get him from the classroom to the water fountain in the hall?" one writer may wail. Or, "How do I get her from Tuesday afternoon to Thursday morning?" another may cry. In both cases, as in most involving transition, the key is directness.

If you want to get your character from the classroom to the water fountain, merely write, "He left the classroom and walked to the water fountain." Or even more simply, "After leaving class he went to the water fountain." Or most simply of all, a sentence in the classroom and the next paragraph beginning, "Later, at the water fountain. . . ."

The point is that you will almost certainly need some transition in your short story—it's a universal ingredient in short story architecture—but it is far too easy to get all fouled up trying to be subtle or clever when a direct and simple statement will almost always do the trick.

In other words, the reader does not *need* a cleverly disguised method of transition. The reader wants to get on with things! Even a wide transition—from New York on Monday to London Tuesday night, for example—can be bridged in a sentence. The reader will follow the character and the plot and couldn't care less about whether you fret about "smoothness" in getting changes made in locale or time.

Sometimes, in longer stories, you can put some of your transitions in the "cracks" — leaving them out entirely and substituting a row of asterisks or a double-spaced gap in your copy to indicate a major break in the action. Often this is done when it's not necessary. If you as the author follow the story, the reader will follow you without complaint. Transitions only become hard to follow when story logic has broken down—and that's another can of worms entirely, as you already know.

Usually at this point in a regular chapter you encounter a concluding summary. These Time Out sections will not have such a conclusion because my aim in presenting these sections to you is not to boil down or sum up something, but to suggest broad views about fiction, especially short fiction, and how it works. Perhaps you will want to record a few observations of your own in your journal after reading this section. As we move along, keep this broader picture of things in the back of your mind somewhere. It may provide the frame into which everything will fit one day . . . the day when you smack yourself on the forehead and see your own synthesis and say, "Of course! It's so simple! Why didn't I see it before?"

## Chapter Five

# Deciding What Kind of Story It Will Be

---

PROGRESS CHECK:

✔ *Have you created a number of character trait/tag cards?*

✔ *Have you (perhaps) begun to think about how some of these cards could be used to create a story character you might actually use?*

✔ *Perhaps you can find a journal entry!*

---

There are as many kinds of stories in the world as anyone can imagine. The variety is almost infinite.

In practical terms, however, it may help you a great deal in laying out your own short story map if you recognize and understand that most short fiction falls into one of three categories: stories of *conflict*, stories of *decision*, or stories of *discovery*. It's important for you to recognize what these types are, and where you fit in.

You may be taken aback by the suggestion that you should "fit in" somewhere in the panoply of possible kinds of stories. Over your career, you undoubtedly will write stories of each major type listed above, plus others that don't quite fit any single category, being a combination of types.

Most writers have a natural tendency to write one kind of story most of the time. They imagine their stories in certain terms, and feel most comfortable writing stories of a given type. (My own tendency, for example, is to write stories of conflict. Hence many of my novels have been categorized as suspense. A few others have turned out to be mainly stories of discovery, as a young narrator comes of age in the course of the narrative. But there's little doubt where I most often feel comfortable.)

It may clarify your thinking about fiction, too, to consider the basic types of story, then consider where you might most easily and comfortably fit in.

## CONFLICT STORIES

In the story of *conflict*, the central character selects some specific story goal, the attainment of which will, he thinks, make him happy. But someone else in the story opposes his quest, and so there is a struggle. In the end, or climax, the two major opposing characters usually have an ultimate face-off of some kind, and someone wins . . . and someone loses.

Note that the conflict does not have to be a melodramatic, action-packed fight, although of course it may be. It can be a goal-oriented struggle of almost any kind. The key to having a conflict, as we define it here, is to have a protagonist with a goal and an antagonist who either wants the same goal or is intent on keeping the protagonist from reaching it. In such a situation there will be give-and-take, maneuver, struggle and tension. At the end of such a story, there is almost always a clear-cut winner and loser.

It is important, in understanding the story of conflict, to be quite sure what "conflict" means. As explained above, "conflict" is a struggle. This is far different from mere adversity.

While a conflict is a fight at some level of intensity, adversity is just bad luck . . . a sickness over which one has no control . . . a sudden rainstorm . . . a tree falling on you as you stroll blindly through the forest. You have little if any chance of really fighting adversity; it simply happens. So while "conflict" means struggle, "adversity" means blind fate.

In a conflict, then, one person strives for a clear goal—and someone else opposes him. Your lead character tries something, and his opponent throws a roadblock in the way.

Conflict is active and dynamic, and your character struggles to resolve the conflict the way he wishes. The reader tends to choose sides in a conflict, and root for the character you set up as most sympathetic. On the other hand, adversity is bad luck, and though we may feel sorry for the afflicted character, we know that such problems are largely a working of fate, over which the character has no control; therefore the same intensity of side-taking does not develop.

Consider it this way: In life, more often than not, we face adversity, or blind fate. The times of real conflict, however, are the most memorable. If you choose to write stories of conflict, you will be dealing with highly dramatic struggle and maneuver, the central character's goal always clearly in mind. While adversity may build sympathy for a character, there will seldom if ever be a real sense that the character is struggling in a meaningful, goal-directed way that the reader can share.

Traditional westerns, most espionage, outdoor adventure, and stories featuring a quest (notably stories such as the Indiana Jones epics on the screen) are usually conflict stories.

Does the distinction between conflict and adversity mean that you can't have both in the same story? Not at all. But it's immensely helpful to remember the difference, because while conflict motivates and moves a story dynamically, adversity is the passive working of fate, and can't do much more than make someone in the story miserable.

To cement this idea in your mind, take out three fresh cards.

On the front of each card, briefly describe a conflict between two characters, some kind of fight. You might, for example, write on one card, "Joe and Bill both claim the bag of gold found in the mine; only one can have it." Or: "Jennifer wants to stay in Rockport, but husband Ralph insists they must move to a new job in Chicago." These are just two quick examples of a possible conflict situation.

Once you have jotted down notes for three potential conflicts, turn over each card and write how the story might involve only adversity.

In the case of the two examples provided, for example, you might write something like, "Joe and Bill find some gold, but then they lose it in a storm." Or: "Jennifer loves Rockport, but husband Ralph's new job means they have to move, and she feels sad."

This small exercise shouldn't take long, but by briefly contrasting a fight on one side of the card and a static, bad-luck version of the same basic situation on the other, you may get a better feel for the crucial distinction being made here.

## DECISION STORIES

With your conflict/adversity understanding strengthened, we can turn to the next major type of story, the story of *decision*. In this type, the central character has a problem that must be fixed or need that must be fulfilled if he is to be happy again. Solving the problem or fulfilling the need requires the character to make a decision. But often he is not at all clear what the exact dimensions of the decision might be. He is befuddled and confused. In the end, having perhaps made several small decisions during the course of the story, he must take some action—make some major decision that may be life-changing.

There may or may not be a clear-cut antagonist in such a story. It often helps to create one, even if the antagonist's opposition is very low-key. Representing the other side of the argument with a story person helps clarify issues for the reader; and at best the existence of this person makes the decision-making process more complex and painful for the main figure.

There may be a strong element of conflict in such a story that is nevertheless primarily characterized by the need for an important decision—whether to move to a new city, whether to take a new job, whether to get (or remain) married. If conflict exists in such a yarn, it should remain secondary to the character's preoccupation with unhappy circumstances and the need to decide something to make things better.

On the other hand, this kind of story may have little or no conflict in it. If the unhappy pressure for a decision is strong enough— the character unhappy enough—then the reader's worry about the upcoming decision will itself give the story sufficient tension. (Sometimes the best stories of all may be clearly one type or the other, yet have the other element dominant in the ending.)

For example, the classic movie *Shane*, although filled with conflict and typical in many ways of the conflict-laden western, ultimately turns on decision: Shane's resolve to take up his gun once more and fight the local thugs. The stories of Henry James and Edith Wharton, among others, are classics of the decision type. Many contemporary magazines carry stories of decision, but sometimes it's difficult for you to spot the decision, or the magnitude of its importance.

As before, you may wish at this point to do a few minutes' work with three more cards. This time, on each card briefly describe a difficult decision a character might worry about throughout a story.

In doing this assignment, be sure to make the choice as specific and clear as possible. *Don't*, for example, write on a card, "Barbara has to decide to make some changes in her life." This is too vague to help you much if you choose to write a story about Barbara. Instead, you might write something like, "Barbara must decide whether to take the new job at the bank, hoping it can change her life, even though she risks losing her friend Jim by leaving her present clerical position." This obviously is specific; it also begins to spell out the importance of the decision in more ways than one.

Pause in reading, and fill out those three cards. (Who knows? As with the conflict cards, one or more of them might go into your shoebox under a heading such as "story types," and later become an idea for a story you actually write.)

## DISCOVERY STORIES

In the story of *discovery*, often the quietest kind, the major character is adrift or puzzled or without clear story goals—or any combination thereof. Finally he comes to some major discovery that has the potential to change his life forever.

This type of story may be extremely quiet and subtle. It may depend more than any other type on style, mood and nuance. It may end up with nothing more significant, objectively, than the falling of a leaf. It's often the most difficult kind of story to write because it is so formless, and depends so heavily on fine writing about deeply felt emotion.

The main character has no clear goal in such a story, and a strong adversary is impossible because there is nothing explicit to fight about. There may, however, be a person who irritates or saddens the major character, and the existence of such an unsympathetic secondary character often provides a feeling of reader uneasiness a bit like that caused by overt conflict; this story person may also add to the lead character's feelings of sadness or need.

The story—especially the short story—of discovery often seems the most realistic of any type because it appears to be unstructured and based on random events like those that often happen in real life. When you read a story by a master like Saul Bellow, for example, you may not be at all aware of how carefully crafted the "wandering" story really is. But such fiction does have a central focus and organizational principle.

Such stories are centered on the lead character's *need* and *preoccupation*, even if the character himself feels adrift. Thus, if you want to write such a story, your main objective in planning it should be to identify the discovery that will take place at the end—what that discovery is, what it comes to mean to the character, and how it can be life-changing. Having done this, you can then work backward to set up the need at the very outset, and keep the character preoccupied with this inchoate sense of need throughout.

To summarize our observations about the types of story, then, we might say:

- The story of conflict is the record of a goal-motivated fight.
- The story of decision is the record of an agonized search for new direction.
- The story of discovery is the record of a pilgrim's blind wandering until a life-changing discovery, perhaps very tiny indeed, is made.

## AN ADDITIONAL ASSIGNMENT

It will be helpful if you will do the following assignments before proceeding.

First, take out several of your own stories, reread them, and see which of the above fiction categories each tends to fit. For each story, fill out a card specifying the title, the type of story, and any weakness in telling or other creative problem you may see that story having.

Try to do this for five of your most recent stories.

You will probably find some elements of each type in your work, even in the same story. You may categorize a story as one of conflict, for example, yet see that a major discovery comes at the end as part of the climax. That's natural.

The point, however, is that you will probably find a pattern—a dominant type—that typifies the kind of story you tell. This will reflect (a) your unexamined assumptions about what a story is, or (b) your basic tendency as a writer at this time, probably founded on your strengths and weaknesses as you perceive them, and the kind of story you instinctively feel most comfortable telling.

If you learn that you have been writing a particular type of short story pretty consistently, based on unexamined assumptions about what a story is for you, then you may want to think about the other types of stories, and whether you want to try to write differently, just to see how it feels to you. If you believe you have been writing a given type of story because that's where your strengths as a writer lie, you should ask yourself whether you want to continue in that groove, or try branching out to improve your skills.

For example, you may find that you have been writing mainly

stories of discovery. Do you feel that this kind of story is the type with which you feel most comfortable? Do you ever yearn to write more brittle dialogue, or perhaps even physical action, into a yarn? Then perhaps you should consciously try a story of conflict.

On the other hand, if you have been writing nothing but conflict, and feel disappointed because you never seem able to wedge observations about your characters into your action-driven plots, maybe you should try consciously to write a story of decision next time. You might discover strengths in yourself as a writer that you didn't suspect.

Whatever tendencies you discover in your own work—or feelings you uncover about a certain type of story—this is an excellent time to continue your journal with a new entry. Try to specify your own story-type tendencies as clearly and precisely as possible. Ruminate about writing an entirely different kind of story. Compare and contrast your recent work with older stories in your files. All such self-analysis stands a chance of bringing new insights into what you've been doing right in your fiction—and what you may have been doing wrong, which is to say, against your natural likes or tendencies.

Having done some of this study, it would be helpful if you took the matter a step or two further. Dig out a handful of published short stories (or even novels will do for this bit of work) that you particularly enjoyed or admired when you read them. Classify them as conflict, decision or discovery.

You may well find that a "pure" type isn't in your list of favorites, in which case you must ask yourself questions such as, "What is the *dominant* type of story here?" And, "If I had to categorize this story as a single type, what word would I be forced to use?"

This work will further clarify your thinking about story types, and your own tendencies.

## HOW CHARACTER AND STORY TYPE JIBE

Hint: It often becomes easier to categorize a story by analyzing the kind of protagonist—hero or heroine—it features. We'll look more at the phenomenon later, but it can be pointed out now that each kind of story tends to draw a certain kind of character into it—or to put it the other way around, a certain kind of character tends to gravitate to a particular type of story.

All generalizations are dangerous, and the following may be more dangerous than most. But here are some skeletal observations about what kind of story most often fits with what general kind of character, and vice versa.

The story of conflict demands a person of action as its protagonist. There must be action in such a story, an active give-and-take struggle with the antagonist. You cannot write such a story about a dreamy, retiring, frightened little mouse of a character; you must delineate a character ready and even willing to *fight* for his story goal because he sees it as essential to his happiness.

Or, looking at it from the opposite end of the creative spectrum, if you want to write about an active, take-charge type of character, you will find yourself almost forced to create a plot of conflict. Put into a quieter type of story, the action hero or heroine will undoubtedly destroy with impatience, go stark raving mad from inaction, or (most likely) destroy your story plans by taking charge and turning it into a quest.

The story of decision cannot function well with such an action-prone character. Here you will need someone more thoughtful, slower to anger, perhaps far less clear about *what* might make him happy. This character is often very intelligent, very sensitive, aware that a problem exists, but unable to see clearly what needs to be decided to make things better in the story world.

So if you have a central figure in mind who is intelligent, thoughtful, and perhaps *hesitant* to take action, you may find it best to cast him into the story of decision. He will not do a lot of overt fighting in the story, but he will continue to meander, desperately trying to find a solution to the bad feelings inside or the bad situation outside, or both. And finally he will come to a thoughtful decision — usually an ethical one — based on everything he thinks and feels.

In the story of discovery, your character quite likely will be even less action- or goal-oriented than either of his brothers in the other two basic types. He will likely be even more thoughtful and more sensitive — very often in more emotional pain, or at least more aware of it because he has more story time to think about it. His uniqueness lies in his self-awareness as a pilgrim — a person in search of something that can change everything for him forever. At the end of his story journey, he will learn something that may be major or could, as mentioned earlier, be as subtle as a falling leaf. At any rate, he will need to be most sensitive for the story-ending discovery to have immediate significance, either for him or for the reader.

Three basic types of story . . . three basic types of character who tend to gravitate to a given kind of plot. In looking at favorite published stories, you may only be able to categorize its general type by studying the kind of central character it has. That's just fine. Studying stories from new angles is almost always useful to the writer during her learning process—something which never stops for any of us.

Not so incidentally, note that all three types of story protagonists will have something in common. They will all tend to have a certain persistence, almost a doggedness, about them. None is a shrinking violet. Each is strongly motivated. They just show their motivation to solve problems in different ways, because they are different sorts of folks. None of them will quit or resign from the story, because they share one thing: the knowledge that *the outcome of this story is somehow vital to their peace of mind, self-respect or happiness.*

In evaluating your own and published fiction, ask yourself how you or that other writer told the reader just how important the story action is to the main character's central happiness. (What's that, you say? You didn't make that as clear in the story as you might have? You may want to fix that story problem right away.)

## STARTING TO PLAN YOUR STORY AND CHARACTER TYPE

Having gotten this far, you have sufficient ammunition for planning the type of story you want to tell next, and the kind of character or characters you will need to get the job done. (Or maybe you will work the decision-making process in reverse, first knowing the kind of story people you want to deal with, and then picking the kind of story that they will function in best.)

Here, then, is the assignment that almost certainly will lead you to a story: Fill out at least ten *character objective* cards. These cards will be used in stories of conflict.

You fill out each card by first listing at the top the name of your central character. Immediately below this, list something this central figure might be willing to fight for.

Some of these story goals might be objects—a new car, a better job, a bag of gold. Others might tend to be less physical, such as recognition in the community or self-respect.

In any case, the key here is to identify the central story goal, over which *there can be a conflict.*

Finally, on the front-side of the card, state in ten words or less why the character wants this goal—why it is essential to his happiness.

Having gotten this far, turn each card over. On the back, put down the name of the character in the story who will furnish most of the opposition—the conflict. On another line below, state in ten words or less why he opposes the main character.

This is a lot of work, but we're just beginning.

After you have filled out the objective cards for stories of conflict—and only then—take the next step: Fill out cards for stories of decision. Again, ten cards, one per story. On the front side, write the character's name, the kind of decision he faces, and why reaching this decision is so important.

On the back of each card, write down why the decision is difficult. This might be a character—a traditional controlling husband, say, arguing constantly that his wife should not even be *considering* whether to start her own law practice. Or perhaps it is a memory of an earlier attempt to make a life-changing decision—and failing to follow through at the last minute due to fear of the unknown.

Finally, make out ten *discovery* cards. On the front, write down the name of the character. Then try to pinpoint the need, or personal sadness, that makes this character so miserable or lost.

On the back of each card, write in a few words a subtle *change* that can take place at the end of your story to provide your character with some sense of discovery . . . and new direction.

None of this work will be easy, and it may be time-consuming. Chances are strong, however, that you will benefit in at least two important ways. So take the time to do all the assigned work up to this point before moving on.

## BENEFITS OF WORK WITH THE STORY-TYPE CARDS

You will derive more than one benefit from the work you have just done on story types.

First, you will probably find one set of cards considerably easier to imagine and fill out. This should give you a strong additional clue as to your forte as a writer of short fiction—the kind of story you may be best at writing.

Second, you now should have thirty story-type cards—the skeletons for thirty stories. Some day you might find that you have delved into the pile and written almost all of these ideas!

What has just happened, you see, is that you have exercised your imagination — the right hemisphere of your brain — as well as the logical left side. This is good practice in itself. And sometimes we get our best creative ideas when, instead of feverishly searching for them, we think we are doing another sort of work. Thus — here — you may have been thinking only of grinding through the assignment in as logical and analytical way as possible. By so focusing your intentions, you may well have let your imagination work more freely behind the scenes, as it were.

It's the same way our best ideas sometimes come when we're driving in traffic, and concentrating wholly on that (we think!), or when we're mowing the lawn or baking a cake. While the objective, analytical part of the mind is busy with a task, the unpressurized creative side can come up with the darndest things unbidden. Like some other aspects of creativity in this book, it's another mystery. Enough to say it happens, and helps us.

There will be other times when I try to trick you into being more imaginative by pretending that your assignment is analytical only. I won't always call such tricks to your attention. They'll be there, and they'll help you.

## SUMMARY

There are essentially three story types: conflict, decision and discovery. They call for different kinds of characters, and satisfy different needs in readers. You should know your tendencies as a writer in this regard, and work hard to complete a supply of cards delineating examples of each type as best you can imagine them.

You should have your basic thirty new cards on story types filled out before proceeding. This may take a while, but every card stands a chance of being grist for a story you will actually write one day fairly soon.

*Chapter Six*

# Deciding How Your Story People Will Look . . . and Talk

---

PROGRESS CHECK:

✔ *Do you have all your assigned cards and notes up to date?*
✔ *Continue to think about the kind of story people—and the type of story—you seem to like best.*

---

I f things have been seeming difficult for you on some of our preliminary work up to this point, it should not dismay you. The feeling of difficulty may only mean that you are absorbing a lot of new information. (My mother used to say that the sting of iodine in a cut meant it was working; it's far more certain that any "sting" you've felt in doing these assignments means that *they* are working.)

On the other hand, perhaps some of the work already done has fired your imagination with a story idea, and you are already working on that as you proceed here. That's absolutely fine, too. Each of us reacts a bit differently to learning material, and there is no right or wrong creative reaction.

Let's press on.

In chapter four, you learned the first steps in effective characterization: deciding the kinds of people you liked and disliked, and why; and identifying physical tags to show the reader as demonstration of the desirable or undesirable traits you had identified. You began building a characterization file, using cards.

In chapter five you took the process a step further by seeing how character type affects the kind of story you tell, and vice versa. Again, you practiced and built your storytelling inventory of materials by filling out cards on different types of characters for different types of stories.

As noted above, it may be that some of this work has already stimulated your imagination with story ideas that you can't wait to write. There's no problem with moving ahead on that. Here we're taking the storytelling process slowly, and step by step, laying out every road on your map. If you choose to wait until all the steps have been laid out for you, and done by you as instructed, that's fine. On the other hand, if something has already made bells ring for you, and you're plunging into a new story even as you continue here, that's OK too because you can always revise if you later learn new ideas and techniques that show you how to improve.

It won't be long now before all your fundamental building blocks—in the form of cards and other materials—begin to fall into place. So we'll continue the step-by-step process regardless of what else you may be doing creatively.

In this chapter we'll take another couple of steps toward building the story you're writing as you study the Map. First we'll look at methods of physically describing your characters; then we'll consider how real people talk—and how your story people must talk if they're to be convincing.

## WHAT DOES YOUR CHARACTER LOOK LIKE?

It may strike you as odd to raise the question of story character appearances here. After all, we already have seen how to devise physical aspects, including things that can be seen, to serve as tags for internal traits. But sometimes the appearance of a person—whether in real life or in a story—may not be a tag for anything, but simply how that person looks. For example, your lead male character may, you decide, be tall and thin. Or he may walk with a slight limp. Or your lead female character may have dark hair. None of these aspects of appearance has much to do with an internal trait. Yet you make it considerably easier for your reader to visualize your story if you provide such hints about how the story people look.

That's primarily what we're talking about here: aspects of the character's appearance that you put in primarily to help the reader identify him or her. Of course some aspects of appearance may also speak to the character's personality, but dark hair, for example, or a slight limp may say nothing except "Hey, reader, here's something to help you remember this story person."

Now, given the fact that you'll help the reader by providing some touch of identifying/visualizing information, it stands to reason that you first need to do that visualization for yourself. It will help you to do this if you remember the following points.

First—always first—you must remember that the soul of the modern short story is *brevity* and tight writing—no unnecessary verbiage. Except in the most unusual circumstances, the day is long past when you could spare even a paragraph in a short story lecturing your reader on how a character looks.

What does this mean? Simply that you must first visualize your character, but then you must seek ways to describe him as quickly, in as few choice words, as possible. If you find yourself going on and on, describing a character, let it be a warning sign to you: You may be writing flabby, ineffective fiction. A rule of thumb might be that you should seriously question any single passage of character description that extends more than two sentences.

This sounds harsh. You may have much more than that to say about how your character looks and even acts. You may choose to come back later in the story and add some other aspect of appearance if you must.

Another angle on this same question relates to how readers visualize story characters. Many readers don't like to be told too much about how a character looks; they want to be free to imagine the character on their own. They will be satisfied with the briefest sketch by the author, leaving maximum room for them to exercise their own imaginations.

Should you leave character visualization entirely to the reader? Actually, some writers do. But most short fiction today contains very brief descriptions I've urged on you here—picking one or two vivid, salient details of a character's appearance, then letting that small detail stand for the whole, igniting the reader's imagination to fill in the rest.

If you're reading with great acuity here, you'll have already seen the problem with such suggestive vivid portrayal. The technique puts a grave burden on the writer to pick just the right single detail (or two) that will fire the reader's imagination to "see" a complete and credible character. This often takes painstaking work.

What do you do? *Observation* of real-life people around you is an important step. I hope you will watch family and friends, and people on the commuter train or in the office, and ask yourself how you would describe *this* person in a story if you had only 20 to 30 words.

What—you should ask yourself—is this person's single, dominant impression? Is it her angularity or roundness? Her brisk walk or her beehive hairdo? Her pallor or her deep tan? Are her eyes striking and important, or is the descriptor her vivid red hair?

Carry cards with you! They'll remind you to make proper observations. Having made such an observation of a person named Sally, for example, you should find or make time immediately, or at least *as soon as possible*, to write the real person's name on a card, then write the 20 to 30 words of physical description that most vividly sum her up.

Some people are relatively easy. Others are subtle. You must struggle with both types.

You may, for example, be dealing with a character as outrageous as Herb, the salesman in the old *WKRP* television series; mention of his checkered bell-bottom slacks, penny loafers and red-striped sportcoat may be almost all you need to set the reader imagining on his own. There is a TV newsman in the local market where I live who seems to have about forty front teeth; if I were to put him in a story, I would say little else about his appearance. On the other hand, your real-life person may be so quiet in appearance that you have to study her with great intensity to learn what is at the center of how she looks . . . how you would describe her to your readers.

It may help sometimes to remember that appearance can go beyond static physical description. Perhaps you want to fill out a card on your aunt, a very quiet, shy woman who seems to have nothing vivid about her appearance. But then you may notice her habit of sitting quietly, hands folded gently in her lap, her eyes off in some private world of thought. The *mannerism* of folded hands might be the detail you need to bring her to life for your reader.

You may find it cumbersome when you start carrying *appearance cards* around with you. But you will be amazed by how quickly they sharpen your observations, making you aware of details in people that you may have never consciously noticed before. The process can enrich your daily life, as well as providing grist for your short-story character mill.

As we go along, we'll discover other angles to character appearance, but the ones mentioned here are the most important. So start carrying cards, making careful observations, and recording thoughts on people.

You should create a new category in your shoebox or filing box, perhaps a subcategory under "characters," if that's what you named a broad category earlier, or perhaps under "real people." Whatever you call it, consider that you have a standing assignment to observe real people and fill out fresh cards.

Some of these cards may become useful to you in your next story. Others may languish for months or years before you find a need for just such a character. In any case this is valuable work.

This does not mean, incidentally, that you will ever necessarily take a real-life person and stick them directly into a story, unchanged. You will find it much more useful to take a little bit of Aunt Helen, say, and a little bit of friend Martha, and combine physical characteristics for a fictional character a bit more vivid than either of them. Or the process of observing and noting real people's appearances may give you a sudden idea for how to describe some character whose origin in your imagination may forever be a mystery to you. In any case, the cards have helped you.

You should check yourself in the future on how well you are following up on use of appearance cards. On your kitchen or office calendar, or in your appointment book, leaf forward a month, and six months, from the present date. On such dated pages, write something like, "How many appearance cards this week?"

I hope you'll find that you've collected a number of such cards in the previous week. But if you find you've begun to neglect your writer's job of acute observation, the note will remind you to start again. It's a vital part of learning to characterize your story people briefly but with verve.

It's not something I or anyone else can check. It's up to you.

## HOW SHOULD YOUR STORY CHARACTER TALK?

In a word—as with description—the answer is: *briefly*.

Long-winded speeches or characters lecturing each other are passé in modern short fiction. When a character says something, it is almost always said to another story person—in dialogue. And while real-life talk may meander and become verbose, short-story dialogue *appears to sound* realistic to the reader only when honed to its suggestive minimum.

Thus real-life talk and story dialogue are often vastly different. In real life, your friend may say something like the following:

"Well, I was thinking about playing golf today, but the wind is up over twenty, which really puckers me up because the weatherman said calm, so what would you think of going out to the mall for lunch, and maybe walk around some, window-shop, stare at the beasties?"

You might note this bit of verbosity on a card, and even plan to use it. When you finally write it, however, chances are that it would be pared down something like this:

"Too windy for golf. Weatherman messed up, and it really puckers me. What say we go out to the mall, eat, walk around and stare at the beasties?"

This example assumes that the phrases "puckers me up" and "stare at the beasties" were the two most vivid and interesting things said by the real-life person.

But what if you thought, standing there listening to your friend, that there was no way you could make his speech punchy and short enough, given the need to hurry on with the story? Maybe you just stood there, slightly bored, as he droned on.

Then you might go a step further, when you used the card you wrote on him, and *break the speech up* — short as you have already made it — by imagining and inserting comments by a second character, something like this:

> "Too windy for golf," Joe said.
> "The forecast said it would be nice," I said.
> "Yeah, but the weatherman messed up."
> "Too bad, Joe. I know how much you like getting out there on the weekend."
> "Really puckers me." Joe sighed.
> "Maybe we could do something else."
> He thought about it and brightened. "Yeah. Go out to the mall. Eat lunch. Walk around, stare at the beasties."

In such a way is modern dialogue often built. The foregoing example is by no means a particularly fetching one — let's admit that — but it does illustrate the process. A reader's eye flies over such passages, so even if they seem to take up extra space, the effect on the reader is one of speed.

So you see how you can take two and possibly three steps to make your character's story talk convincing: First, you observe real people, and make notes on cards.

Second, you pare down and sharpen what was really said.

And third (sometimes) you interpolate another character's brief comments, interruptions or questions to break the dialogue into briefer segments.

In any case, all such verbal observations should be put on cards which can go into another subcategory right alongside your appearance cards. You may name this subcategory "dialogue cards" or something similar. And, again, part of your job is to work on observing real-life situations with greater attention to detail, and writing your observations on cards as soon thereafter as possible, filing the cards for future story use.

## SPEECH PATTERNS AND TYPES TO AVOID

In their quest for the kind of apparent realism just described above, some writers lose control of their material and allow verbose meandering, or otherwise forget that dialogue springs out of real life, but is seldom literally taken from real life.

A prime example of erring by trying to be too realistic can be found in the area of grammar and syntax. Hearing real people drop the final *g*'s of their words, or say things like "gummint" for "government" and "didna" for "did not," the unwary writer in search of realism drops all kinds of weird phonetic spellings and grammatical monstrosities into her copy. This is almost always a mistake.

The reasons are twofold.

First, the use of offbeat spelling and grammar tends to draw the reader's attention to the strange language at the same time it distracts the reader from content. In other words, the reader tends to get hung up on how something is being said by a character, rather than on what is being said, and possibly why it is being said.

Second, the use of "funny" spelling and grammar puts you the writer in grave peril of being mistaken. Some readers will jump to the conclusion that you are sneering at the character who so speaks, or holding him up to ridicule. This is most often the case when a writer attempts to render a regional dialect or ethnic pronunciation pattern. Such attempts are almost certain to fail, and carry the added risk that the writer may be seen as a bigot or even a racist.

The moral: When confronted with a real-life person who mangles words and the language, be very careful of trying to put such atrocities into your story people's talk. At most, select one or two inoffensive mispronunciations or malapropisms, and let those examples stand for the entire speech pattern. (The reader will pick up on such verbal hints if you make them vivid and characteristic, and more would not be necessary even if the dangers just cited did not exist.)

In real life, too, as noted earlier in this chapter, people tend to ramble, repeat themselves, lose the conversational thread, and make long-winded speeches. You may suggest all of these real-life tendencies in some of your dialogue. The key in all cases is to devise the shortest possible example of what you're trying to illustrate, and let that example stand for the much more verbose whole. If you wished to illustrate that a certain man in your story was a bag of wind, for example, you might have him make a five- or six-line speech, preferably pontificating as he does so, very early in his introduction in the story; this five or six lines would *look like* a three- or four-minute speech in the real world, and would be enough to give the reader a clear "listen" to how that character must sound.

## IMPROPER USES OF DIALOGUE

Finally, there is something else you must remember as you make dialogue notes on cards and later translate them into story examples. That is simply this: Dialogue should not be used merely for the writer's convenience.

By that I mean you should not have story people talking just to give you a way of introducing facts into the story, and you should not devise speeches for them as an easy way for you to describe something.

We've all seen clumsy examples of dialogue in which the writer did not create realistic talk, but instead just put quotation marks around some factual exposition or description. Something like, "Well, hello there, Charles! My, my! You're wearing a dark suit which looks good on you! And don't I see a healthier glow on your face? Is that a result of that new health spa program you told me about a week or so ago, saying the special membership offer was too good to pass up?"

Another improper use of dialogue, usually much more subtle, is the writer's use of story talk to tell things about character feelings that real people would never so openly reveal. So we have characters in stories who walk up to the barest acquaintances and spill their deepest feelings, volunteering things about themselves that no real person in his right mind would ever so openly divulge.

A rule of thumb is that if a character is to blurt out something of deep emotional significance — a really piercing revelation — it should come only under the worst kind of story pressure, and when the character emotionally is *in extremis*. Characters who casually tell their deepest feelings for the writer's convenience are never believable.

If you find yourself falling into this kind of dialogue trap on occasion, and can't come up with a strong story development to *force* such an emotional revelation from the character, it is far better to provide the reader with a brief glimpse into the character's psyche through introspection, a direct statement (again, brief!) that simply says in the most heartfelt way you can imagine, how the character is feeling at the moment.

Such direct attempts at describing emotion are dangerous — the threat of a "purple patch" of sentimentality — and they may also get out of hand in terms of length. Your job is to recognize when such a passage is mandatory for the clarity of your story and the reader's contact with the emotional life of your character; then you must find ways to say it briefly, vividly and without hysteria.

If in reading other people's work you find some of these dialogue abuses, it might help you to take note of it, paste the offending passage in your journal, and try to rewrite it there in a more proper and convincing form. Consider that still another assignment!

## SUMMARY

How your story people look and talk is crucial. You can best get ideas for both by observing real-life people and situations. To assist in this process, the wise writer carries a supply of filing cards at virtually all times, makes acute observations, and records his impressions on a card as soon as possible after the observation.

Physical descriptions of your story people should be as brief as possible. You should seek the short, vivid, suggestive wording that gets at the essential center of how a given character looks. Given the right clue, the reader will visualize the character for himself.

Similarly, in handling story talk, brevity is of the utmost importance. Observation of real-life speech patterns will provide ideas and inspiration. But it is then up to the writer to condense and sharpen these to suggest the reality, not transcribe it.

Your supply of story-possibility cards, in terms of descriptive observations and speech patterns, should grow daily. The sharpened acuity of observation that they encourage will make you a better writer. The new cards you collect will give you material for many characters in many stories.

## Chapter Seven

# Picking a Place for Your Story

---

PROGRESS CHECK:

✔ *By now, your shoebox filing system should have several dozen cards (at least!) in five to eight categories and subcategories.*

✔ *Do you have this system working well and continuously in order to build the habits of a good writer and provide yourself with a growing accumulation of story materials?*

---

With your story tendencies becoming clearer in your own mind, and with a stock of story ideas and other observation cards growing daily, it's time for you to make the other crucial decisions necessary before you can put it all together and write your best story ever.

Many decisions must be made soon. But one of the most important has to do with where your story is to take place.

Do you usually know your story setting as well as you should? Please take out some fresh cards and give yourself a simple test about the setting for the story that you're planning, or for the last story you wrote.

On Card No. 1, write the general geographical location—the United States, for example, or Europe, and then a more specific location, narrowing your locale to region of a country, state or province, county or similar political unit, city or town, and finally neighborhood.

On Card No. 2, provide the skeleton of information you know about your setting at this point, things like the following: What specific sensory details clearly typify or identify this setting? Is it mountainous, for example, or flatland? Is it near water? Is it loud or quiet? What do the trees (if any) look like? Is the neighborhood rich or poor? What other salient details can you provide in a word or two?

On Card No. 3, identify the *feeling* of the setting you are using. Is it all sunshine and joy, for example, or filled with rain and dreariness? If there are mountains, do they contribute a feeling of majesty, or do they hang over the town like ominous weight? (You may vary the emotional tone of the story in many ways other than with setting—and the feeling of the setting may even change in response to plot developments that affect the viewpoint character's mood. But here we are trying to identify the pervasive story feeling that your setting tends to set up.)

On Card No. 4, explain how your lead character or characters are "children of this environment" — or how they are out of place in it, perhaps even at odds with it.

On Card No. 5, write down anything about the setting that you may have guessed at—anything that requires further research.

On Card No. 6, write down what you conclude from this quick self-examination. Do you need to think about how character and setting fit or fight? Do you need to look up some additional facts?

In your journal, make a brief entry reflecting your understanding of how setting can affect a story and the people in it. You might also record any insights about setting and its importance that this small exercise brought to your attention.

## THE MANY VALUES OF SETTING

Story setting is important because your reader must be able to visualize (at least in a general way) where your story plays out. To be convincing, your fiction must transport your reader into a physical universe that he can imagine vividly. Once transported into that setting, the reader is set up to believe everything else more readily because he is already out of his day-to-day environment and imaginatively in your "story world."

For this and other reasons to be pointed out in a moment or two, selection and presentation of setting must not be a casual matter. Far too many writers consider setting an afterthought, or an unexamined assumption, and then compound their error by failing to research the setting or to present it in the most vivid and convincing manner possible. So as we go through this chapter of decision-making, remember a basic fact: *The writer must know her story setting well, or everything else in the story may fail.*

I hope that, knowing this, your professional pride would always motivate you to handle setting with care for accuracy and detail.

But there is one additional practical reason for doing so. If you publish a story in a mass-market publication, and make a factual mistake of any kind, you can be sure that an astonishing number of readers will spot the error. Worse, some of them are sure to write your publisher, complaining. What do you suppose this error-induced complaining will do to your chances of getting another story accepted by the same publisher?

As mentioned above, readers need physical description of the story setting to visualize and "enter" the plot action. But selection and presentation of setting is important for other reasons as well.

As briefly implied at the start of this chapter, the setting of your story will tend to determine the kind of people you can realistically use in the story, the feeling and mood of the story as it grows out of the physical setting, and some of the attitudes and problems that the story people may subscribe to or experience.

For example, it would be difficult for a reader to be shown a traditional western/cowboy setting, then be presented with a character whose value system more closely resembles a contemporary urban teen. By the same token, it would take a feat of literary genius to make millions of readers laugh in a story set vividly inside a nursing home, and featuring a dying old woman. If you set up a traditional western setting, the reader expects western-style people and attitudes: independence, boundless optimism based on the existence of an open western frontier, and (sadly) a belief in Manifest Destiny that justifies a racist attitude toward Native Americans. Similarly, a nursing home setting is almost sure to be sad.

You should take a few moments now and consider setting, and ask yourself a few questions. The following list is suggestive and not comprehensive. Work to develop more setting questions on your own.

1. Are my story plots cast in the most convincing setting? (That is, does the story action fit the setting, or might some other setting be better for a given story?)

2. Are my story characters truly "children of the story environment," or have I thoughtlessly stuck the wrong kind of story people in a given setting — or, conversely, have I created a setting in which *these* story people would not normally be found?

3. Have I researched my setting to avoid obvious errors?

As stated, you will think of many more questions if you work at it a bit. Whatever observations you may make should be noted in your journal.

Setting is such an important aspect of the writing craft that I have devoted an entire book to the subject: *Setting* (Writer's Digest Books). We can't cover everything here, but a few more salient points need to be made.

## SELECTION OF STORY SETTING

In general, as you pick a setting for a given story, you have two broad possibilities: You can write about a place you already know well, such as your hometown or your workplace for example, or about a fictional place similar enough to what you know that you are already comfortable with setting details. Or you can write about a place and time that you have never experienced *but can research.*

There are no other options. You cannot guess.

Now, it might seem that using a familiar setting—your hometown or office or a favorite vacation spot—would require no work on your part. In terms of physical appearance and generalities, this could be true. But let me suggest that you take some time, before you have turned beyond this chapter, to inventory the facts you really have in hand about your "familiar" environment. Can you answer such questions as:

1. What is the form of government (or management)? City manager? Mayor? Town council or town commission or some other term? If writing about an office, what is the formal title of the general supervisor? Is the company privately held or owned by stockholders?

2. How large is the town in square miles?

3. Is it typical of the region or unusual, such as perhaps a college town or one-industry area dominated by that single entity?

4. What demographic data do you have? Consider population, average income, etc.

5. What is the single dominant landmark in the area?

6. If an office, what is the general mood of the workforce? Satisfied? Nervous? Unhappy? What?

7. If you had to write a paragraph establishing the feeling and mood of this place, what would that paragraph say?

8. If you needed to do so, what single physical aspect of your setting would you choose as a sort of symbol of the whole? Would

you focus on aged houses under brooding, spooky old elm trees, for example, or the happy faces of children leaving grade school in the afternoon? Would you choose a sunny day or a rainy one as a general indicator of place-tone?

9. If you were asked to write a paragraph by the area's greatest admirer, what would it say?

10. If you were asked to write another paragraph telling what the area's worst and unhappiest critic might say, what would that paragraph contain?

This list is suggestive only. It is designed to make you think more deeply about that familiar story setting that—perhaps—you have taken for granted.

You have been given many card assignments already, so this time let's make the work optional. Consider the sample questions listed above (and other similar ones you may think of). If you conclude that you don't know as much about your "familiar" setting as you may have imagined, ask yourself this additional key question: If I choose to set a story in this "known environment," does the type of story I tell demand that I learn more to make my setting convincing?

Now, it may be that your favorite kind of story, as determined in earlier self-evaluations, is the type that focuses sharply on the inner emotional life of a character (to the exclusion of many specific factual details about the setting). Or you may realize by now that your forte as a writer is the story of an isolated character whose "world" is the inside of a small house. Or your short stories may, almost always, cover a limited time span and focus narrowly on a single incident or argument so brief and intense that there simply is no time or story-space for detailed description of setting. If such a circumstance truly defines "your kind of story," maybe you don't need to worry about deeper or broader details of your familiar setting.

If, on the other hand, your favorite kind of story needs a strong political background, or sharp physical detail to provide a certain mood, or fine detail about a business or profession, then you may have to look deeper at the story environment you earlier took for granted as familiar and well known.

If *this* is the case, some additional card-work may be in order. Identify the kinds of additional information you need, whether it is historical, political, demographic or whatever. Each area of information should be written atop a card, which will become a category card. Your next step is to come up with as many specific questions as possible for each category of information, and write each specific answer on another card.

You might, for example, realize that you must know more genuine history of your immediate region before you can write one of your favorite kinds of stories, a tale of ambition and setback in the early part of the century. You might then fill out a category card listing "county history." Under that category you might fill out additional specific questions cards such as:

- What was the population in 1900?
- What was the main business of the town?
- How did people get around? Horseback? Rail?
- Where were the town or city limits?
- What building or buildings dominated the downtown?
- Was today's local newspaper in existence then? (If so, find a copy at the library or historical society and look at it for "flavor." If not, what was the local news medium?)
- What clothing styles were popular at the time? Find pictures.
- What were prices like? Study ads of the time.

And so on! Your list probably will be much more helpful than mine, because it will be tailored to your own kind of story and its needs.

Your conclusion from all of this work may well be that you didn't know your local area as well as you thought, and that creation of a credible setting is seldom as easy as finished stories make it appear. This should not be dismaying to you; after all, by becoming aware of a need to improve your stories, you have just taken the first step toward repairing things in that area. And by the time you have finished asking new questions, you are ready to take the final important step, which is: Cards in hand, go out and find the answers.

The same kind of general approach will be even more necessary, of course, if you determine that you want to put your next story in an *unfamiliar setting*.

The prospect of learning enough about a faraway place or time, or perhaps an unfamiliar work environment such as a hospital or big corporation, may be daunting at first. But there is seldom sufficient reason to give up on a story idea because learning about the right setting would be too hard. There are many sources of information.

Again, you may wish to become more familar with some of the most obvious information sources nearby. On cards, perhaps you should write some of those possible sources, then plan to investigate them.

Most areas, for example, will have many of the following for listing on possible source cards: public library, newspaper files, historical society, genealogical society or club, school library or records, museum, reference books available through interlibrary loan, bookstore, local authorities, or—last but not least—the post office.

You will be pleasantly surprised, once you have identified specific needs and questions about some faraway place or business, how readily experts or public relations persons in that unknown place will furnish you with information if you simply write a letter and ask. You should never feel shy about writing letters, seeking setting information. Many large-company and government offices exist in large measure to handle such requests. They will be only too happy to help you, or perhaps direct you to some other source where they know the information will be available.

Identify your needs and possible sources, and don't be bashful! Make this work another card project.

If you have access to a computer database, be it Prodigy or CompuServe or the Internet, you will naturally turn to that enormous research tool.

Finally, please pay particular attention to another item listed in the sources above. That is your *local authority*. Be sure to ask around, at church, at school, at the office, at the library or wherever, seeking any local citizen who might have expertise in the factual area you need. And note that this does not have to be a potential source of only local information! You may have one of the world's recognized students of Tahiti (or of copper mining, or of anything else) living on the next street from you. Never take it for granted that your only good source resides a thousand miles away. You may, after asking around, be pleasantly surprised.

## HOW TO PRESENT YOUR SETTING

Once you have defined your setting needs and have collected all the necessary information, factual and descriptive, you are ready to plan how to use the data in your story. In doing so, you should remember your ABCs—Accuracy, Brevity, Clarity.

"Accuracy" has already been explained. You must never guess

about a setting detail, and you must provide such detail if it is essential to your story's believability. In collecting material for possible use as part of the story's setting, you will most likely have ten (or a hundred) times more detail than you will ever use. You will also have checked your sources at least twice to make sure that setting detail tucked away on a $3'' \times 5''$ card is absolutely accurate.

This is true not only because of the need for story credibility, but because modern tastes demand brevity—which includes the briefest and most economical introduction of setting material into the story. When you are working with certain facts, and have confidence in your accuracy, you can best hone your wordage and give the reader "just the facts, ma'am." It's when you try to guess, or write around an area of factual uncertainty, that you tend to get verbose.

So you will be accurate and brief. But in addition good research will help you be clear. If you know, for example, that the drug Cordarone is a very powerful tool in treating irregular heartbeat, then you may be able to use the drug name and explain it with great precision and clarity. But if you know only general information— that such drugs exist—you may have a devil of a time being clear about what that flat, pink pill is doing in the story.

Before trusting to fate that your setting information is accurate and capable of being delivered in the story with brevity and clarity, test yourself again. Pull out any and all cards you may have about the setting of the story you're planning to write next. From these cards, select the ones you consider most important.

Now turn each of these crucial fact cards over, and write on the back the simplest, most direct, most accurate and most evocative brief statement about this part of the setting that you can create, just as you would write it into your story.

Again, you may find that you need more information. You will also be exploring the feeling of the story setting, and its most salient characteristics. And as a bonus, when you get to creation of the story, you won't be so likely to hang up on how to phrase what you already know.

## PLANNING HOW TO WRITE IT

Determining the best way to say anything in your story will be part of your lifelong creative quest. But in terms of your description of setting material, it may help you to remember that there are essentially three ways to present setting to your reader: by direct description, by simile or by metaphor.

Detailed discussion of such stylistic questions is beyond the scope of this book, which is after all a *work*book that defines working systems rather than esthetics. But since almost all information about setting is delivered to the reader in one of the ways just mentioned, a brief look may be helpful.

Most often you will likely tell the reader what your setting looks like, or feels like (or whatever) by describing it directly. Thus you might write:

> The nearly vertical side of Mount Daisy stood over the small western town, keeping it in shadow during all but the middle of the day.

This is direct and straightforward, and there's nothing wrong with it. On some occasions, however, you might want to help your reader visualize more strongly that "vertical side of Mount Daisy" by reverting to a simile, perhaps something like this:

> The granite face of Mount Daisy stood close behind the town like an enormous, cruel stone prison wall, designed to hold the townspeople in forever.

Similes of this kind, usually using the "like" such-and-such construction, tend to convey more than physical information. It's likely that the reader of a passage such as the one immediately above will think "prison" or some equally unpalatable idea, every time the mountain is mentioned thereafter in the story.

Sometimes, of course, the simile is less emotionally loaded, and is used merely as a visual or other imagining-aid for the reader. One might write, for example, that "the landscape looked like a scene shot on the moon." (Isn't it amazing, in our day and time, that some earth setting might be best suggested to the reader by a simile arousing memory of television pictures from our moon.) Here, except for a possible feeling of bleakness, it's unlikely that the simile does more than compare an unknown setting with one more familiar to the reader, for clarity.

When she employs *metaphor* to aid in describing a setting, the writer usually is after an effect much like that provided by simile, but sometimes with even more emotional punch. Here a comparison is not drawn, an actual object or place being said to be something else; here a symbol stands for the actual object.

Returning to our old western town, we might say in metaphor:

> Mount Daisy reared a grim, gray prison wall over the town; but the wall held no doors of escape . . . no dream of parole or pardon.

Finding different methods to describe setting can be a challenging task that frees creative ideas. Before concluding this chapter — regardless of other voluntary work you may have done earlier — consider this an assignment that will help you in the long run:

Whatever setting you have in mind for your next story, fill out at least six setting-orientation cards for it. Pick the most salient feature or features of the setting, and fill out two brief cards using direct description, two using simile, and two using metaphor. Then file these cards. They will turn out to be much more than practice. If you do this work carefully, and with thought, at least two or three of the resulting cards will end up being useful in your story as you write it.

Here is an additional assignment that will make everything clearer. Go through two published stories with your colored pencils, searching for things said about the setting. Bracket physical descriptions in *black*. Then go through and mark sight-description words in *red*, hearing impressions in *blue*, odor impressions in *green*, taste impressions in *yellow* and tactile sensations in *purple*.

Study your markings and take note of which senses this author seems to favor. Is this characteristic of most fiction? Is any sense entirely left out? Do you think it is overdone? Record your observations.

Go through the story again. In a different color, mark any statements of fact about the setting. Also, looking for any statements about the setting that characters may utter in dialogue. Again, analyze and record your observations.

Now analyze one or two of your own stories. How do they compare? What do you conclude? Force yourself to come to some conclusions by way of comparison and contrast. Try to see your own tendencies better in this regard.

Do you find direct description? Simile? Metaphor? Mark some of these in your own copy. Could you strengthen your handling of setting by using more of one kind or another of these?

## SUMMARY

Proper handling of setting is vital to making your story real and believable for your reader. You must know your story setting well, and there are many local and national sources of information, so you never need to rely on guesswork.

*Concise*    Accuracy, Brevity and Clarity are the ABCs of work with setting.

You may present setting detail directly, as simple description, or you may use simile or metaphor. It's possible that you'll use all three methods in your next story.

You should have *at least* a few new cards dealing with setting before you turn to the next chapter. Some assignments in this chapter were optional; others were not. And any time you skip an optional assignment, you should do so only after sincere self-examination — and certainty that you won't later wish you had done this preparatory work.

# WHAT MAKES PEOPLE TICK

*survival*
*bills*
*social*
*faith all*

S ometimes it's easy enough in real life or in fiction to understand what makes people tick. Ramona's father dies and she
weeps. Or someone breaks into Dan's store, stealing everything, and Dan is angry and depressed. Or Bill loses his job,
so he goes out looking for a new one. In a great many cases, it's
easy to understand the motive behind the action—and the person
behind the motive.

The deeper one can look into human nature, however, the better
she can draw moving and believable characters in a story. The ideas
about human behavior and motivation that are most directly appli-
cable to the Map approach to short-story writing are included in a
number of work assignments in a number of other chapters. But
here might be a good time to step back a bit and consider some
theories of personality which enter into our work program only
indirectly, or by inference. They're as much a part of a writer's
assumptions about short-storytelling as anything else presented between these covers.

Most writers are at least slightly informed about three theories
of the human personality: the classic Freud, the stimulus-response,
and the Transactional Analysis.

Admittedly none of these is as directly helpful to the writer as is
the idea of the self-concept, which we'll put into practice in chapter
ten. But a basic understanding of these will set the stage for your

work in that later chapter, and give you an overview that might stimulate new thinking on your part.

So let's take a brief and very simplified look, a sort of long glance that may suggest some new direction of study for you.

## FREUD

We couldn't cover Freud's approach to the human personality if we used the whole volume, of course. People have been studying and explaining Freud's ideas since he first introduced some of them, and the study and explanation is far from over. In terms of the writer, however, one of Freud's concepts that may be the most helpful is that of the subconscious or unconscious mind.

I hesitate to discuss any Freudian concept in the simplest terms because it may be that you know more about it than I do, and could consider my oversimplification a disservice. However, I can be brave and try anyway, just to clarify what can help the writer create characters.

The concept in simplest terms is that we are made up of two minds or functioning mental processes, the conscious mind and the unconscious mind. The conscious, obviously, is the thinking and feeling of which we are aware. If I feel bad today and realize I have just caught a cold, and remember that a certain cold medicine has helped in the past—and then go to the store and buy some of that medicine—my actions have been based on a conscious thought process. On the other hand, if my wife sends me to the grocery on a chilly day when I don't want to go, and I later begin to get a cold, *maybe* my unconscious mind resented my willingness to do a dreadful chore, and retaliated by weakening my immune system and giving me a cold. Or maybe I find myself doing something for *no* reason I can think of, and am forced to admit that possibly there is stuff going on in my head of which I am not aware.

Freud, of course, liked to point to word-mistakes as a sign of the unconscious at work. I might hate to go to the grocery alone, but I tell my wife, "Of course. I don't mind going to the cemetery—I mean *grocery*." Or she might then tell *me*, "Why don't you make yourself feel better at the grocery by buying yourself some of that candy that makes you so fat—I mean *happy*?"

The point need not be pursued by way of explanation. The significance to you as a writer, however, should be obvious. In motivating your characters, you can sometimes create motive and resulting action that the character himself might not fully understand.

A young woman, for example, could go deeply into debt for a new dress when she can't afford it, then might say in your story, "I don't know why I did that!" To make this work, however, you as the writer would have to understand her unconscious mind and realize that something just reminded her of her dead mother, who always bought her a new spring dress at this time of year.

Will explanation of unconscious motivations in a story have to be brought out clearly at some point in the telling? Sometimes yes, sometimes no. Often the logic of the unconscious is so resonant that the reader will understand and believe when even *he* does not fully understand at the conscious level. But this kind of instinctive and profoundly felt understanding will only come if you have thought long and deeply about the character — her past and present, and all her identifiable feelings — in an attempt to understand much more about her unconscious mind than she herself ever will understand.

On the other hand, a total acceptance of the power and wisdom of the unconscious mind carries with it a danger. The writer might become so enamored of unconscious motivation that she begins writing stories based too strenuously on the unconscious alone. Then her characters might start doing all sorts of outlandish and unexplainable things, and the author might reply to criticism of motivation by paraphrasing the line used by a TV comic in years past: "The unconscious made her do it!" The key here is moderation in using unconscious motivation, recognition of its possible power, and the need for the author to understand the character's unconscious motivation even when the character doesn't.

To put this another way, the unconscious mind has a magnificent logic and potency all its own. Just because we are not aware of it does not mean that it is not *there*, driving much of our lives. We can use this knowledge in creating credible and complex characters in our short stories. But behind every use of the unconscious in fiction must lie an incredible amount of hard work by the writer to plumb the depths of the imagined person's unconscious. Why is the character the way she is? What is her unconscious mind assuming and thinking? How can seemingly contradictory aspects of her personality be explained by reference to the unconscious?

We can't just plead that "the unconscious made her do it!"

One further note about the unconscious mind that may seem to fly in the face of almost everything presented here in the Map. Many of our motives as writers — especially with reference to the birth of our story and character ideas, and the kinds of stories we tend to write — may stem at least in part from our own unconscious.

I remember once, for example, after one of my novels had just come out, I thought it was quite different from anything I had previously written. My daughter, about fourteen at the time, read the new book and asked me bluntly, "When do you think you will be finished working through your problems with your father?" Stunned, I realized at once that there had been a father-son relationship somewhere near the heart of my last five books. My unconscious mind had driven me to return again and again to this theme until *it* was satisfied the problem had somehow been worked through.

This is not a matter about which to be overly concerned. But if you find yourself "stuck" with writing a particular kind of story, or if you find that you just can't seem to get on with some story on which you've already lavished considerable effort, you might want at least to consider the possiblity that your unconscious mind is trying to tell you something. Maybe this isn't the right story for you to be working on at this time. Or maybe it's time for you to make a conscious effort to change your creative preoccupations.

I can't begin to guess what thought about the unconscious mind may do for you, but I urge you to think about it. At the least it may help you analyze and deepen some of your characters. At best it could give you self-awareness that could change more than your writing career.

## BEHAVIORISM

Turning to the stimulus-response explanation of human behavior, we enter simpler territory. Often (and I think misleadingly) referred to as "behaviorism," this theory is not only simpler but considerably more mechanical in terms of explaining who we are and why we do what we do.

In the simplest terms it says you poke an amoeba with a microscopic probe, and the amoeba shrinks away — stimulus and response; so you provide a human being with a complex of stimuli in childhood, or even prior to birth, then "poke him" with another stimulus later in life, and he reacts in some way to the whole complex in a pattern that is mechanistic and pre-ordained—again, stimulus and response.

This is appealing because it is so simple. At the same time, most humans find it repulsive to suppose that even our most complex thinking is the mere result of neurons firing in reponse to stimuli . . . that ultimately there is no free will . . . that even self-awareness is a by-product of our being poked just like that amoeba.

Wherever you may fall in your estimation of the theory, however, you can use it very simply in your study of story characters and plots. The principle is twofold: When you want someone to do something in a story, be sure to provide an immediate (as well as longer-term background) reason for doing it (a stimulus). Whenever you put down on paper a meaningful event, a potential stimulus— be it a death in the family or a sudden summer rainstorm or a kind word—always remember that the event *must show results* (a response) in the story.

To put this another way, you can prod characters along by giving them a stimulus. And if you give them a stimulus, they can't just sit there; they must react.

This simple idea can solve a multitude of seemingly complicated plotting problems for you. Figure out what you want, and contrive a cause. Figure out what you've already set as a cause, and decide what the response ought to be.

It will not, incidentally, result in behavior as mechanical as it might seem to threaten. Each of us is different. Each story character is different. Present each of us with the identical stimulus and we may react quite differently. In other words, awareness of stimulus-response theory does not make character behavior predictable; all it does is possibly make it more believable on an immediate, superficial level. Every character can be shown to have free will—unlike the theory held by the sternest believers in behaviorism—so that between the stimulus and the response can be character thought that determines what that response will be, and why.

## TRANSACTIONAL ANALYSIS

Moving along to transactional analysis and how it explains human behavior, we come to a school of thought less "mystical" or abstract than the Freudian approach, yet considerably richer in complexity than behaviorism.

The body of theory involved in TA, as it is usually called, stems from the methodolgy of study. Transactional analysis got its start with the idea that a person's motives and rationale for behavior could be made clear, both to others and to himself, through setting up interaction with others—group therapy, if you will—and then analyzing the kinds of transactions the person characteristically and even habitually worked through with these people.

After analyzing many cases involving such group interactions, the founders of TA came up with a theory that sounds a bit like Freud's theory of id, ego and superego, but which is really quite different because it deals only with motives that are accessible to the conscious mind. In other words, TA analyzes things that Freud's ego or conscious mind would recognize.

TA states that the ego part of every person is composed of a parent ego state, an adult ego state, and a child ego state. We behave, TA says, largely depending on which ego state is in control at the moment—which has been "cathected."

So a person who acts impulsive, petulant, playful, silly or scared is in all likelihood "in his child" at the moment. If another person comes over and tries to comfort the "child," it's likely that that person is in her parent. If a third party stands by, cooly analyzing the situation and drawing intellectual conclusions from it, then he is probably in his adult.

To put all this another way, the child ego state is composed of those feelings that existed in the very young and largely emotional-spontaneous child. The parent ego state emulates parental behavior as generally accepted: It is the caretaker and provider. The adult ego state is sort of like the computer that watches over things—including internal dialogue between parent and child—and draws logical conclusions and acts from an objective analysis of the data flowing from the internal dialogue or from the outside.

All of these ego states, remember, can be brought to consciousness with the right analytical assistance. (It's characteristic of the TA group approach that a person may go along for weeks, interacting with others and feeling she is learning nothing. Then suddenly she sees herself acting in a way she recognizes as habitual—which can lead to a blinding insight into one's own ego state functioning and possibly faulty ways of relating to others as well as to oneself.)

The fact that all ego states are said to be admissable to consciousness is a very important factor in TA theory. It says, in effect, that while a person may not be conscious of their motives and thought-patterns *now*, they can realize them at any time. And this in turn implies that you as a writer can work out motives and patterns of thinking for your characters depending on what ego state you choose to place them in at any given time in the story.

By way of example, consider the following.

Suppose you have two characters, Mabel and David, in their apartment. You need to stir up an argument between the two of them. You begin the scene, but Mabel seems to be analyzing past events in a dispassionate manner, and David insists on calmly agreeing or disagreeing— but in no way picking a fight. The two remain maddeningly cool—as they were conceived usually to be in the story—but right now you need a squabble.

Resort to your knowledge of TA theory. Put one of them in their child ego state, for example. The child is mercurial, emotional, unpredictable, and quick to scream or cry or attack or run away. *Now* if the other person remains in his or her adult, the one in the child ego state will get very frustrated because the adult responses will seem cold and even nasty.

So Mabel, let's say, is in her child when the scene begins. She sobs and bemoans her fate, going over the same data she presented in the earlier, failed version of the scene (when she was in her adult). Now David responds as before, from his analytical adult. Mabel stamps her foot, throws a vase at him, and screams something like, "You don't care at all how I feel! You're horrible!" David replies calmly again, at which point Mabel gets more furious. David slips from adult into child, and starts shouting names at her.

*Now* you have a conflict going, and all because you knew enough to put one of the potential combatants in a disharmonious ego state.

## Life Script

There is another bit of TA theory that can help a writer greatly in planning a character's feelings and present motives, and that is the idea of a *life script*. Again this is something that can be figured out, but most people never manage to do it.

What the life script theory says, in simplest terms, is that we decide very early in life what kind of person we are going to be, and what kind of life pattern we are likely to follow—and then we follow this usually unrecognized script even if it takes us to our doom.

Suppose, for example, that Billy as a very young boy heard his father berate him over and over for failing to pick up his toys or finish the food on his plate. "You try but you never succeed," Dad yells at him. "When are you going to start doing things a hundred percent right? Sometimes I think you never will!"

At which point the child Billy takes his father's words as Gospel, and unknowingly accepts Dad's observations and predictions as an accurate map of the territory ahead. Father's thoughtless words are taken to heart by the child, and later becomes the child ego state as other aspects of his personality develop. So what would a character be like in your story if you imagined this kind of life script for him?

His script would be to try . . . but never quite succeed or feel he is acceptable. He might almost be imagined as wearing a sweatshirt with the motto "I always try" on the front, and the words "but I never quite make it" on the back, where he can't be aware of them. So he would go through school trying to make As . . . but never quite making them. He would work hard at his job . . . but never quite be the top man. He would marry a nice woman, probably . . . but always feel down deep that she probably really can't love him a lot because he's always been . . . a screwup.

You can make your characters have all kinds of tragic or superficially unexplainable personality problems by devising life scripts that have some hidden, lethal component. Indeed, many great stories could flow from your word processor as you created a life script for a character and then wrote about his desperate quest to figure out what's wrong that can make him so unhappy.

On an even less complicated level, suppose you have a character in your story who is always cold and logical—maddeningly so. It may help you portray him to realize that he is always in his adult, and lacks the personal capacity to allow either of his other ego states to assume dominance over his feelings and behavior, even for an instant. Or you might have another story person who constantly runs around caretaking others; won't it expand your view of her to realize that she is constantly in her parent, perhaps while the unrecognized adult inside struggles to set up logic to her life, and the hidden child cries because she never gets to play?

You may wish to take some of the simplified concepts presented in this Time Out section and study them further. The self-help or psychology section of your library or bookstore is probably crammed with books that take off from one or another of these theoretical bases. Or you may feel that you have enough here, and start working on some aspects of your planned characters along the lines intimated herein. In any case, I hope the brief presentation of these additional thoughts about what makes people tick will broaden the framework into which your ultimate perception of writing will fit.

*Chapter Eight*

# Setting Up Your Map

---

PROGRESS CHECK:

✔ *Have you thought carefully about your story setting, and what you may need to learn before you can present it?*

✔ *Are you continuing to observe real people, and make cards that will help you create credible, vivid composite characters?*

---

E arlier it was noted that some readers of the Map may have already been "turned on" by the discussion and early card-work, and might be deep into writing or rewriting a short story. As noted then, this is just fine because anything done now can be revised later if necessary.

Now, however, a word might be addressed to another possible part of the readership—the aspiring short story writer who has become dismayed or even discouraged by all the suggested decision-making. I can almost hear a wail of unease: "I didn't know it would take all this work to write one short story. It all seems too hard."

If you happen to feel a little like that right now, I hope you will take heart. Much of the work suggested up to this point is the kind of thing that (a) you will do only once as self-inventory, or only periodically in your career, or (b) the kind of work that will prove so helpful that it will soon become second nature to you, a part of your newly productive and rewarding methodology for creative work. Furthermore, from here in your blueprint for writing an effective short story, our pace quickens and you move ever nearer to that planned, finished story—the best you've ever written.

## DOING IT THE EASY WAY

As I mentioned at the outset, some writers sit down to work on a new story with nothing more than vague inspiration. They figure out everything as they write. That's fine, if it works for them, but as I noted before, such an approach is a very hard way to write fiction. And the longer the story, the harder it will become. Writing a novel, or even a novella, on impulse-inspiration alone is impossible for most of us, and often almost-endless revision is the only way to salvage such a project . . . if it can be salvaged at all.

It's far easier, most professionals agree, to plan ahead and get it right the first time. Although all writers revise their work before letting it see the light of day, revision is never the most pleasant task, and the more things wrong with the initial effort, the harder revision becomes. Our aim here is to have a total program designed to make things far easier than they might be if you wrote when— or if—some burst of inspiration momentarily motivated you to start putting down some words that might end up being "fixable."

This chapter will take you through a great many questions that you should be able to answer clearly before launching into that next yarn. Although the list may appear formidable, you should remember that it's the *easy* way to set up a story, making crucial map-making decisions before the fact, rather than in the desperation that can come when you get partway through a story and find yourself stuck.

I'll assume here, as I've assumed from the beginning, that you want to write more than a plotless mood piece or vignette. It seems that most people can occasionally dash off one of these brief literary accidents, and most people, unfortunately, have. Thus the marketplace is overloaded with short bursts of inspiration that go nowhere and mean nothing beyond a sigh or a feeling that the prose is pretty. In this book we're dealing with a longer story with a definite plot of some kind, as outlined in chapter five.

You'll need to round up more blank file cards, then start through the list of questions that comprises the bulk of this chapter. You don't necessarily have to fill out a card with your answer to each question in the exact order in which it is presented here, but you'll need to come up with an answer to all of them sooner or later; so unless you get badly hung up on a given question, you might as well answer them in the order listed.

This point of taking the assignments in the order listed, incidentally, brings up a question about writing that is often asked at writers conferences: "Do I have to write the story straight through, beginning to end, or can I skip around and write whatever parts I feel like, in whatever order the idea comes to me?"

The answer, of course, is that you can write a story any way you wish. But it must also be pointed out that some parts of any story are more fun to write than other parts. Very, very often, the big, most-fun-to-write scene is the first idea that came to the writer; it is in some ways the scene or incident or paragraph of feeling for which the whole story is written.

You may like to jump in and write a draft of such a "hot" part of the story as it now exists in your imagination, and this might give you an additional emotional boost. But you should avoid writing all the "most fun parts" first. Why? Because you might use up all your most passionate feelings about the story and then be left with a seemingly insurmountable job in producing the harder parts that fall between the highs.

Most writers tell me that they always have some wonderful scenes or passages in their minds when they start. But usually they force themselves to start writing at the beginning, taking one thing at a time, so that — in a way — they write the hard parts of the story to get to the part or parts they really ache to write. "If I wrote all my big scenes first, and out of story order," one writer put it, "I probably would never finish a story. I write to *get to* the high points — the easy parts." (Needless to say, perhaps, this same principle of taking things one step at a time, in order, lies behind the whole approach in this book.)

I hope, then, that you will try to write answers to the following questions in the order given. You should have one question per card, one answer on the back, or on a separate, numbered sheet of paper.

This assignment, unlike some of the earlier ones, is to be aimed specifically at the story you are now beginning to map. To say this another way, all your answers to the following must fit into the same story.

As you work through the list, you may find that you're forced to go back to some earlier narrative decision as listed on an earlier card, changing something to provide internal story consistency. To give an exaggerated example, if you decided early that the story was to be set in the year 1776, then later realized that the plot could be worked out *only* by reception of a fax message, you would obviously have to stop and figure out a way around use of the fax, or go back and change the answer card that said the story was to be set in 1776. Similarly, if you decided earlier that your main character was a seventy-year-old man, then later decided that you simply had to have him in a two-mile foot-chase at the climax, chances are you would go back, reexamine your decision about the hero's age, and make him younger and perhaps more athletic.

These, as I said, are extreme examples, but good plotting often requires reexamination of early assumptions about the story that are not much more subtle. It's only when you get stuck halfway through a story—and feel committed to the erroneous line you may be on—that things seem deep and complex. Fundamentally changing stories is hard; changing cards is easy.

You may find these questions difficult to answer the first time you try this assignment. The imagination doesn't like discipline, and you have little practice with the Map technique. Fight your way through! Before long you will be like most professional writers, asking yourself these and perhaps other similar questions in your mind, without recourse to a printed list. This is called problem-solving.

And what you'll come away with is a list of ingredients that will work in your story—a recipe for your tastiest fiction stew. You'll also be well along to having the tactical, structural map laid out for the story you are almost ready to begin.

## DEFINING STORY ELEMENTS

Here, then, are your work questions:

**What kind of story is it to be?** A romance, perhaps? A mystery? An action/adventure? Science fiction?

This question is not designed to make you follow any kind of formula or pre-ordained story pattern. It is designed to start you thinking even more seriously about the general type of story you want to create, and also thinking about some of the needs (or no-no's) such a story inevitably will carry with it.

A few examples may help.

If you decide that you want to write a science-fiction story, for example—or if that hazy idea has many science-fiction characteristics—then it's pretty certain that you're going to need either some scientific data from which to extrapolate or some space-opera-type action to carry the reader along. If you want to write a romance, it's pretty obvious that you'll need a couple in the story, and some problem keeping them apart. If you decide that you want to do a historical story, you must be sure that answers to later questions don't involve modern appliances or intellectual concepts. (She can't get the news on TV in 1690, obviously, and she can't talk about sexual harrassment: not by that modern term, even though she may suffer it.)

**What is the setting?** Again, a decision here may affect many later ones. For example, the character in a story set on contemporary New York's lower east side is not the same character to be found in a 1930s small town in middle America. Everything ties together in an effective story; that's why we work with the cards: to make sure.

Further, in terms of this decision, you should consider setting materials as advised in chapter seven. If you see that you are going to need additional material on the setting you want to use, you should fill out one or more additional cards, listing the questions you must have answered.

**What is the time period of the story?** Again, will other aspects of the story fit this time period? Are there things about that time period that you must research for accuracy—and a credible story?

**Who is your main character?** In a preliminary way, at least, answer several specific questions about him, such as:

- What is his name?
- His age?
- His occupation?
- His background in brief?
- His appearance?
- Anything else about him that is unusual or vital to the story?

In regard to this preliminary decision-making, we must, of course, have answers that are consistent with all the other decisions. It will not be necessary at this point to know *everything* about the character, but you should make decisions on at least those facts listed above. If you aren't sure about something—his name, for example—remember that you can always change it later; for now, give it your best shot.

One more proviso: If you find yourself noting that he has an "average" background, or "average" looks, it should be a warning flag for you. People like to read about characters who are something other than "average." You should force yourself to imagine some interesting thing in his background . . . some aspect of his appearance that takes him out of the crowd.

**What is this character like, in a general way?** Describe the kind of person he is, perhaps adding a tag to illustrate one or more traits. Here you may well delve back into the trait and tag cards you created earlier, and duplicate some of the information here—or even improve it. In addition, ask yourself such questions as, "How would I explain to my best friend that she should *like* this character?" Or, "If I had to explain to someone what kind of person this character really is, in twenty words or less, what would I say about him?"

**In the story you plan to tell, what does this character see as his problem?** What does he lack or want? What's the problem in his life? How does he feel about it?

**Why is it so vital to this character to reach his story goal,** or come to some new decision, or find some new insight? (What *is* the goal, or what does the decision entail, or what will the new discovery/ insight be and mean?)

**If there is to be some overt conflict in your story (and I hope there will be), who is your antagonist or "villain" character?** In other words, who is going to oppose your main character, standing between him and his goal? Name this character. Think about him.

**What is this villain character like?** (Refer to your answer to the same question about the protagonist.)

**What is this villain's plan?** Specifically how is he going to fight or try to thwart the protagonist or hero? Does his plan make sense? Why and how?

**Why is it essential to your villain's happiness to fight the hero,** or persuade him to make the wrong decision, or prevent his discovery that might lead to new insight and contentment? What makes this antagonist tick?

This may seem like an obvious question, going as it does to a major character's motivation. But a very common mistake in short fiction—given its demand for extreme brevity—is the failure to explain why the antagonist in a story is doing whatever he or she is doing. Too often the villain appears to have *no* reason for his actions, and so is incredible. It may be in real life that people seem to act as they do for no reason. But since fiction has to be better than life in some ways—usually has to make more sense. It's imperative that the villain have better reason to fight the hero than simply the idea that the villain is a bad person.

One of the most difficult planning decisions you have to make may go to this point. You may have to think deeply about the kind of person your antagonist is—his or her background (short-term or long-term), the history of any earlier relationship between protagonist and antagonist, or even some cause of inevitable friction that you might imagine in the setting (such as a town's historic inability to support more than one grocery store, when both characters want to operate one).

To take this one step further, the key words in the questions immediately above may be "essential to happiness." It is not enough for the villain to be nasty by nature. It is probably not enough simply to say the villain has always disliked the hero. You should go that extra step and ask yourself, "Why will the antagonist be much happier if he can win this struggle? Why is the battle worth any effort the villain might make?" From such questions credible motive develops in your story plan.

One additional note on this matter: It is barely possible for you to get too logical in your thinking about motivation. As hard as you may work to make a character's motives logical and credible, you must remember too that fiction is about *emotion*. Strong feelings sometimes make real people—and story characters alike—something less than rational. But even when a character may be confused or erratic, you the author should be able to look deeper into that character, sometimes saying something like, "Here is why this character is so consumed by hate or jealousy—is even irrational at the moment." You have to know your villain better than any psychologist ever knew a client.

**Which secondary characters might contribute to the story?** How many do you plan to use? Who are they? Why are they necessary in the story?

In short fiction it is deadly to throw a character into the story just because you happen to consider that character colorful or interesting. There is no time or space for such self-indulgence. Every character must pass the acid test. You need to ask yourself: If this character were not in the story, would the story still work?

To put this another way, secondary characters—except for the incidental taxi driver or doorman—must have impact on the plot in some way. They must support or attack the protagonist or antagonist, or they must serve as a sounding board for one of the major players, or as a person whose presence or activity complicates life for one of the majors. If you look closely, you will notice that even an important secondary character — perhaps the love interest for the protagonist — usually also functions as her confidante, her advisor, or active partner in the struggle; he is not there simply to be interesting or potentially helpful; he is active in some way, and his existence has a bearing on character feeling and thought, or reader understanding of what's going on, or what somebody does next to stir the plot along.

You should give thought to all secondary characters with these facts in mind. Then you must ruthlessly eliminate "speaking role" characters who don't pass the function test.

For the character or characters who pass this test, you should be sure to fill out trait and tag cards, giving this work extreme care. Secondary characters, because they are sometimes onstage very little, may have to have even sharper tags for traits than do major characters, who will be onstage longer, giving the author more time and space for their development.

Such minor characters will not, in all likelihood, have the real depth built into the major characters. But a single sharply identifying tag — always whining, for example, or always slamming things in anger — may make them *appear* deeper than they are, and with great brevity.

**What is the time frame of the story?** Is the action to take place in an hour? A day? A week? In this regard, you should strive to make the time frame as brief as possible; every time you stage a major time transition in short fiction, the intensity of the story experience is diluted for the reader; caught in a brief, engrossing scene, suddenly the reader is asked to jump forward a day, perhaps, and even to another locale; such mental transitions ease story tension for the reader and may even allow his attention to wander — a deadly possibility.

Remember that generally speaking the background of a short story may be very long indeed. Your yarn may represent the climax of a family feud that has gone on for generations, for example. Often your first inkling of a story covers months or even years. But your job as a short story writer is to find a way to boil this down to the briefest possible time frame.

The professional starts her short story's present action as late as possible — as near the climax as possible in present story time. She ruthlessly collapses time for the sake of brevity. So, though you may begin by imagining a story that extends months or even years, you will almost certainly come out with a better and more engrossing short story if you can find a way to tell only about a final day in the saga, or perhaps a few days.

This decision-making process on story time may require you to fill out a number of planning cards. For example, you may end up with two small stacks of cards, one stack delineating all the "back-story" — history you must know, but which you will not narrate in more than a sentence or two—while the other stack may represent two or three scenes that you definitely know you will "play" in far more detail for the reader in present story time. Such planning will help you decide what must be told, and what can be implied or ruthlessly condensed. Making such decisions now will greatly simplify writing the first draft of your story.

**How (and when) does the story start?** Remember that modern readers are impatient. The story must start as arrestingly as possible—and as late in the going as possible, so that pressure on the character is already intense . . . emotion already at a high level.

**How (and when) is the story to end?** In other words, how do you plan to set up the story's climax? Will it be a dramatic physical struggle atop a tall building, perhaps, or a thought that comes quietly with the falling of the first leaf of autumn? Where will it take place? Who will be there? Why? What happens exactly? When does it happen—and here you decide not only the day and the time but the time in relation to the story opening. (As stated above, the closer the beginning and ending may be, the more cohesive and compelling your story is likely to be.)

This question obviously represents a lot of thinking and decision-making on your part. Perhaps you should have a major decision card for "Ending," then describe the ending briefly on that card. Behind it you might have any number of cards further defining the ending in the most precise terms possible, and answering some of the related questions listed just above. If other observations or questions occur to you, then of course you could have cards on those items, too.

Having done all this work, consider one more question: What is the ending going to mean?

This sense of meaning may not be entirely clear to the characters in the story. In one kind of story, the climax is, in effect, a realization or change of feeling. In such a story, it is vital for you to pinpoint the precise meaning of developments, an intellectual insight by the character, perhaps, or a very sharply defined new emotion. But in another story, the characters may come to an obvious conclusion of the action, yet be left with the feeling that they have much yet to work out . . . need time to figure out the total meaning of whatever just took place. Modern short fiction often deals with such ambiguity.

Whatever the characters know or don't know, however, the author must know more than they do. You must know exactly what the ending means, and how the characters feel at such an ending. In addition, you must know precisely the feeling you wish to leave with your reader as a result of this ending, and how it is presented.

For example, let's assume the ending of the story leaves your viewpoint character alone, saddened but determined to carry on. You might have a series of cards on this. Some of them might read like the following.

(Major card for "Ending"):

Joan stands alone in her living room, looking out at the snow; it is Tuesday; she sees a child playing in the snow, and knows she must go on.

(Secondary cards):

1. Time is 4 P.M., and early winter nightfall is near. It's now twenty-six hours since the story present opened.

2. She's alone; Ted just left.

3. The child she sees is four years old, chubby in his snowsuit, laughing and having fun on his sled.

4. She sheds a tear, but then sees that the little boy is a sign of the future.

5. She decides she will go on, struggling to find new meaning in her life. She thinks briefly of some of the good things in her life.

6. Possible wording: "She saw him tumble down the slope and jump right up, chubby in his snow-covered suit. He didn't cry. She wiped the single tear from her cheek.

"She would not cry either."

7. Meaning: Joan has conquered her grief. We all must go on.

Your own cards may be more elaborate, of course.

**In addition to information about your story setting, is there any other factual information you may need for this story?** If so, what is it? If you fill out a card or two specifying factual needs, how do you plan to get that information?

**Can you set this story up so that it "plays" in two or more dramatic scenes,** where the characters interact onstage in the story "now"? If you had to make this story into a stage play, could you do it?

This examination of your story planning is necessary because far too many short stories fail on account of too much character introspection and not enough action. Introspection can be a big part of any story. But if some of the interior thought can be "staged" dramatically in some way, your reader may become more enthralled and involved in the story's tension.

**What will be the viewpoint in this story?** Which chararacter ultimately is the sympathetic hero or heroine you want the reader to identify with? Can this character be at all the right places at the right time so the reader will see all the vital story activities through her eyes?

This question assumes that you realize that most short fiction today is told from the single, isolated viewpoint of one character inside the story action. It is possible to tell a story from the panoramic viewpoint of a god-like observer, but readers generally have trouble developing sympathy for anyone in a story so told. Fiction works best when "in viewpoint."

Your first thought about this question may be that you can't stay in a single viewpoint because "Joe won't know about the wreck, but the reader has to know—so I have to change to the viewpoint of the highway patrol trooper." Or, "Sally doesn't know, but I have to let the reader know that James is writing her a letter she'll receive tomorrow." In almost all cases, such thoughts are fallacious. Always remember that what *you* the author know is not at all what the reader has to know. The reader will find the story more believable, as a matter of fact, if he knows only what the central character knows. That, after all, is the way we live our real lives.

In other words, you must resist the natural author's impulse to make sure the reader knows everything. If it means changing viewpoint from the central character, such an impulse is almost always misguided. Stay in viewpoint and work for reader involvement.

This, of course, makes selection of your viewpoint character even more vital. If you haven't yet decided where the viewpoint should be, ask yourself who the reader will most like and "root for" in the story. Ask yourself who *you* most like and care about. Then decide to put the viewpoint in that story person, make a note on a viewpoint card, and begin to think about how that character's viewpoint on things may be unique and most sympathetic.

**If all goes well, which publications do you think might buy and publish this short story?** Pick up numerous magazines at the store. Note the kinds of stories they publish, the length, kinds of characters used, setting and time frame. Make notes on Market cards defining what a particular magazine seems to like.

## SHEDDING BAD HABITS

It could well be that the listing of these questions seems an enormous task. Or perhaps you already routinely make most of these decisions ahead of time but do not formalize the decisions on note cards. In either case, once again I want to urge you to do the work, laborious as some of it may be.

If you have never considered some of these planning questions before, you have had bad or careless fiction-writing habits. If you have thought about these things before but made no attempt to organize your answers, then again you may have been working out of a bad habit pattern. The only way to shed bad habits is to do something different. That's sometimes painful, but it's the only way.

As I urged you before, take your time working through decision cards in conjunction with this chapter. By the time you have cards in all the suggested categories, you will have a much clearer idea of what your story is about—the beginnings of a real short story map. And let me assure you again that making these decisions will never be as difficult as it may be the first time you make them.

## SUMMARY

If you wish to make the actual writing of your story as simple and straightforward as possible, you will make as many major decisions as possible well ahead of the actual writing—and you will commit those decisions to planning cards.

*outline*

These cards should reflect decisions that are internally consistent with one another.

It's perfectly fine if you get partway through the decision-making process and discover some problem that requires revision of some earlier cards. Revising a card is far less painful than getting stuck halfway through the draft of a story and being so confused you don't know what to do.

## Chapter Nine

# Making Sure Before Moving On

---

PROGRESS CHECK:

✔ *Have you carefully made all the decisions suggested in chapter eight?*

✔ *Are you satisfied with most of them?*

✔ *Did any of this work suggest reworking any earlier cards, such as the one on setting, perhaps, or kind of story?*

---

T he last chapter was a dense one. It asked many questions and asked you to make or reexamine many decisions.

In such situations, we sometimes feel pressure, and respond to that feeling by hurrying too fast.

Recognizing that danger, let's slow down a bit and talk more about some of the most important items we've mentioned—and make darned sure we didn't go through some of them too fast to get maximum benefit from the work they entailed. And let's be certain that no major misunderstandings have crept in. The principles we'll look at will be stated in somewhat different terms, and under major headings that may clarify these principles.

## THE NEED TO BE SPECIFIC

You'll remember that you were asked to decide what kind of story you plan to write. Suggested possibilities were fairly specific. If you categorized your desired story with some precision—as a romance or a western, for example, or even as broadly as a psychological study or something similar—you did well.

If, on the other hand, you wrote something like "mainstream" or "contemporary," you did not think deeply enough about this question. Using a broad term to describe your desired kind of story lets the analytical part of your mind off too easily, and could signal a lax or self-indulgent attitude toward your work. Even worse, if you don't have a sharper idea than that of what you want to write, you don't really have general guideline for further research and planning.

Although many markets claim they don't print "category fiction," what they usually mean is that they don't like to publish *pure* category—a predictable western shoot-'em-up, for example, or a typical romance in which boy meets girl. But most magazine editors have a fairly specific idea of what a story is for them, even if some of them deny it and claim to be totally eclectic.

The moral: The more precisely you can define the type of story you plan to write, the easier it may be to focus your efforts toward the potential strong points of such a story. It doesn't help you much to think about writing a "mainstream story," but it might help clarify your thinking quite a bit if you defined your desired story as "a romance for young readers," for example, or "a detective story." Not only will you tend to pick story people, setting and plot elements that fit this story type, you will think about some of the clichés of this type of story—and work to avoid them.

If you used too vague or general a term to define your desired story, give it further thought and revise your card.

Your examination of story type may help you identify other vital points, which may require reconsideration. For example, does that violent scene you wrote really fit in a love story? Now that you've seen the points discussed, our clarification here may help you work further toward that "synthesis" we talked about in the first Time Out.

## SETTING AND HOW IT MAY AFFECT CHARACTER

Remember that *setting* may have to do with more than physical place. It may also involve the time frame of the story. You need to be aware that the time setting of your story may have a great impact on the kind of story you can tell in the limited space of a modern short story. A story set in the days of the American revolution will almost certainly be seen as a historical, for example; readers of historicals expect detail on dress, customs, recreations, transportation and the like. It's just as true that a story set in 1968 America will probably have vastly different details about attitudes and clothing than would the same basic plot set in 1984. You may wish to reexamine your time setting with these observations in mind.

Setting and character must correspond. Your character should be of the type typically found in your chosen setting (a doctor in a hospital setting, for example). Sometimes your setting may slightly predict your character types. Or to put this another way, the character will seem typical of that setting, and will be relatively comfortable in it.

If your character is *not* in harmony with the chosen setting, you'd be well advised to change your plans for either the character or the setting *unless* the discord between character and setting is a basis for the plot—an innocent man finding himself in a maximum-security prison, for example, or a young woman from New York City getting lost in the Rocky Mountains.

Look again at your setting and character cards, and be prepared to make modifications if you find that you hurried your earlier decisions and made some bad choices.

## SELECTION OF VIEWPOINT

In picking your main character, as you so recently did, you had to be sure the character was central to the action—could be in all the right places at the right times, inasmuch as he is almost certain to be the viewpoint character. You also made sure, I hope, to define an *active* character, a doer. The passive central character is horribly difficult to write about. Again, review your decision cards to make sure your planned hero is the kind of person who will take action, struggle, try to regain happiness.

Look back at your cards and notes, and make sure you're putting the viewpoint in the right person. Watch with special vigilance for a viewpoint character who witnesses the actions of others and never really gets into the middle of things herself. Such observer viewpoints almost always fail, because as many writers have observed, in good stories the viewpoint character *will become* the affected, centrally involved character, or the centrally affected character will somehow take over the story's viewpoint. It's very seldom that you find a viewpoint character who sits and waits; even in a story of discovery the viewpoint character will be doing *something*.

## SELECTION OF GOAL

Review your decisions about goals. Make sure they are listed on your cards as specifically as possible.

Remember that you have to consider the goals of both the protagonist and the antagonist. If either is not motivated toward a goal, there can't be much story tension because they have nothing to struggle about.

"Wanting to be happy" is not specific enough. Selection of character goals is at least a two-step process: picking the very specific short-term goal, then figuring out exactly why this would make the character happy, or at least more comfortable.

### Game Plan

Equally important to specifying the goal and reasons for it is devising some sort of game plan for the character in this story. It isn't enough for him to want a new job because his present one doesn't pay enough. If you have an active character, he or she will come up with some kind of plan to make things better, even in a subtle story of discovery. In real life we sometimes drift and are acted upon by events. But in fiction it is much more satisfying to the reader if the character acts upon events, trying to control his own destiny.

Lack of a character game plan is one of the most common problems in amateur short fiction. Do your your cards reflect an awareness of this principle? Can you chart a series of steps the character either lays out in his mind at the outset of the story, or ad libs in reaction to events as they develop out of his earlier steps?

## KEEPING IT SHORT IN TIME

It's easy to be too gentle with yourself in deciding the time frame of a short story. Enough stress can't be placed on having the shortest possible time frame. Look back at the chronology of the story you plan to put on paper, ruthlessly weeding out earlier events that might be considered backstory. Remember that you seldom err by starting the story as late in the imagined action as possible.

Now, it may be that you heard this advice, but went on and planned a story covering weeks, months or even years. Please reconsider! There is always a way to condense story time. The danger of the long time period is not only dilution of story tension, as mentioned before, but the temptation for the author to lapse into fat paragraphs of narrative summary—sometimes necessary, but never as involving for the reader as dramatic action, onstage, now.

## CONTINUING RESEARCH

Continue to look for needed information—and continue to question yourself about what *additional* categories or types of information you need to add as part of your quest.

It's not too early, incidentally, to start to develop an entirely separate card file for names, addresses and telephone numbers of persons, offices, institutions and agencies where you can access particular kinds of information. This card file should be divided into subject categories, some subjects being somewhat general ("weather information," for example), and some more specific to the kind of story you expect to write most of the time. Since I often write suspense, I have several files just on "armament," divided further into categories for handguns, rifles and shotguns, automatic weapons, knives and "big stuff," a category that includes the name of a man I can call if I want to know more about the cockpit of almost any modern jet fighter.

## WORKING ON YOUR SCENIC PROGRESSION

Finally, a suggestion about the future of our project. I've already suggested that you think hard about ways to tell your story in discrete dramatic scenes. I hope by now you have many such scenes noted on cards.

By all means continue to work on this process as we move along, possibly laying out your cards on a work table, then arranging them in story-chronology order, then filling out other cards outlining or suggesting a method of making the transition from one scene to another . . . then possibly changing the scene cards around, trying them in different order here and there, possibly to build suspense, possibly to make something clearer or withhold a clue or motivate a character in some way.

Don't let your first set of cards "be enough," and don't stop shuffling the cards in search of a better and more dramatic sequence of events in the story. Sometimes the tenth shuffling of card order—or the addition of a single card suggesting an additional scene or fragment of a scene—will make a world of difference in the finished story.

As you do this work, you will begin to have an even clearer understanding of why the cards are such a good idea for story planning. Their portability (and replaceability, if necessary) makes them easy to arrange and rearrange, replace or modify. And as you shuffle, new ideas will flow.

## ADDING CHARACTERS

As you go along, don't hesitate to start placing key character cards under various scene cards, your card for the antagonist being laid out under the card outline for scene two, for example, if that's where the antagonist makes his first appearance. All such arrangements help you see the flow and structure of your story more clearly—will make the final writing infinitely easier.

You may think of other areas where you hurried a bit, or got distracted, or weren't satisified and promised yourself to go back later and try again. This is the time to reconsider everything, and make all the "fixes" and additions.

## SUMMARY

Many of the earlier decisions could have been made too quickly. You should reexamine all your planning to date. A few suggestive reexamination questions were posed in this chapter, but you may think of others as you review what you've done.

As you reexamine your decisions, study the flow and structure of the story now beginning to take shape. Scene cards may be laid out in the order in which they will "play" in the story. Character or research fact cards may be arranged under the various scene cards. Transitional material may begin the planning stages.

The story has begun to assume definite shape. Clearly this is no time to rush ahead without serious consideration of every point.

*Chapter Ten*

# Testing and Deepening Your Characters

---

PROGRESS CHECK:

✔ *Have you reexamined decisions made in chapter eight? Are new setting and character cards still flowing into your files as you do research or observe real-life people for their dominant impressions?*

✔ *Has a clearer idea of your story begun to emerge as you arrange and reshuffle cards?*

---

R eaders often ask whether writers start with plot or with character in developing stories. It's the kind of question most writers can't begin to answer because plot ideas tend to spring forth with characters already in them, and characters usually spring out of the imagination with some of their plot problems already nagging them.

To put it another way: Good plots involve vivid characters, and good characters are always involved in a plot that tests their mettle.

We've made a great many plot decisions in the previous two chapters. Some attention has been paid to characters, too. But now it's time to test our thinking about our story people and devise ways to deepen them, making them more vivid for our readers.

This is the final major planning step we will take before starting to put everything together in the final blueprint for the story you are about to write.

## FINDING THE DOMINANT IMPRESSION

You can never do too much to create vivid characters and cast them against one another in an enthralling setting. So before moving into the later stages of our short story map, let's take a brief look at earlier work, and carry it a step or two further to make our characters better.

In chapter four you identified good and bad character traits, and then assigned one or more physical or behavioral tags to show the internal trait or traits to the reader in the most convincing form. I have asked you since then to continue your observations of real-life people, hoping you would keep these important aspects of characterization in mind as you filled out additional cards reflecting subsequent observations.

Now we want to make sure the traits were as sharply defined as possible, and that the assigned tags were as good as you can make them.

In the earlier assignment, for example, you might have decided that an admirable trait for a sympathetic character would be "kindness," and perhaps you showed as a kind trait the habit of baking cookies for friends, or helping to deliver food to shut-ins as part of a volunteer program that they call "meals-on-wheels" in my hometown. That was fine — then.

In good fiction, however, even the short-story character requires somewhat further development. Rather than showing one simple tag, the convincing character must be built through a variety of tags proving the same trait. Think of these varied tags as "tag clusters."

Thus the woman designated as "kind" would not just bake cookies or drive a volunteer vehicle. You might show her smiling at a friend and patting her on the back in an encouraging way, even though her own day had been sad. You might show her sending a get-well card. You might show her sending flowers to someone, or befriending a small child in the neighborhood, or adopting a kitten, *or virtually all of the above.*

You must wave your tags often. But to avoid reader boredom, devise tag clusters that appear different, even though they are essentially the same.

Thus what you need to do right now is go back and dig out those character trait and tag cards you filled out as an assignment for chapter four, along with any others you have filled out since then. For at least the three characters you most enjoy thinking about now and might use in the same story in the not-too-far-distant future, you need to devise additional tags — in tag clusters — and list those on a new card that you will clip to the original. A very few words or phrases will suffice to describe each new part of a tag cluster further clarifying and developing the trait that heads the original card.

How do you make sure that your additional tags and clusters are the most fitting? The best way is to imagine your character entering your story in the most revealing and characteristic way you can dream up—even if the revealing, characterizing action has nothing to do with whatever plot you may be tinkering with. Write this entry in a few words, or as briefly as possible, making it as vivid and arresting as you can. Now ask yourself the following question: What dominant impression does this character make with this entry? That is to say, how is this entry the perfect illustration of this character's most overwhelming impression—the thing that would stand out most about her if you were just introduced to her in real life? Is she vibrant and saucy and electric with energy, for example, or does she slouch into the story, sad-faced, drab, perpetually tired? Does she enter carrying cookies for a friend, or do we find her sitting alone behind closed draperies, hoping no one calls because she hates the world?

The difference between tag clusters and dominant impression is that tags are the physical clues to traits, the combination of which forms the personality in some hierarchy of importance. The personality trait or traits that stand out most about the character form the dominant impression.

Thus dominant impression is seldom a simple matter. But it gives you an additional tool in devising tags and tag clusters: Having figured out the precise impression you want the character to make, you may find that you need to identify additional traits—and tags for those traits—to make the entrance as dramatic and convincing as possible.

Go back through your cards, then, and atop the second tag cluster card for each character write the dominant impression you wish that character to make. Do this in as few words as possible—perhaps three or four adjectives. This is something you should do right now, before proceeding.

## MAKING CHARACTER COMPARISONS

Finished revising and adding to the cards for at least three (and we hope more) story characters? Good. Let's move on.

The next step involves comparing the characters you have just planned. As suggested earlier, we hope that some of them will be in the same story. With that assumption, it's axiomatic that they can't all be the same kind of people. We need contrast and variety.

Therefore you have to examine the work you just did, asking

yourself the following questions: Are the dominant traits as listed for the various characters clearly different from character to character? Clearly, a story with three "kind" characters, doing the same sort of stuff, won't have as much potential for drama as a story featuring one kind character and one meaner than Scrooge.

If you find that you have inadvertently planned two or three characters with similar traits, tags and dominant impressions, you should realize that your story will turn out "gray," without enough character contrast, and probably with much less potential for drama or conflict than would a story with vastly different kinds of people in it.

Remember we're talking about character *types*, not background or any other factor. You might have three story characters outlined who are all hometown products, who are all accountants, and who all work in the same office, for example, and that might be fine if they are different kinds of people. On the other hand, you might have a cast containing an old man, a young woman, and a precocious child, and if all of them were "kind" in dominant impression, they might be identical dramatically.

Go through the cards. Using colored pencils, mark each major trait in *red*, each tag or tag cluster in *blue*. Make sure the tags are the best you can possibly come up with for the desired trait.

To help yourself further, use the pencils to mark up one published story in the same way. Are there any conclusions you might draw from this analysis of published fiction? Is the published writer dealing with this matter in essentially the same way you plan to deal with it?

Are your tags and tag clusters as listed different for each character? Do you have strong, specific tags? And do they correspond to different kinds of character behavior? That is to say, do you have tags of appearance, habitual activity, personality quirk (such as a facial tic or cracking one's knuckles, to name two horrible examples), speech habit (such as using the same phrase over and over in dialogue)? Have you thought about the kind of habitat that surrounds the character—such matters as the kind of car she drives, how her house is decorated, how she dresses, the kinds of magazines she subscribes to? Attention to this matter—the use of different kinds of tags, perhaps within the same cluster, can greatly enrich your character on paper.

Finally one additional question you should ask yourself: Have you named the character yet?

If you haven't, now is the time to do so. If you have, remember that the character's name may become an important tag in itself. ("Do I really want the kindly old woman to be named Fifi Renee? Do I want to retain the name of Percy Pinkley for the harsh, crude male character in this story?")

As before, if you spot any inconsistencies or needs in this category of your story planning, this is the time to fix them. This may take a while, but it's better to do it now than later, when other matters should have much more of your writing attention.

## RANKING THE CHARACTERS IN YOUR CAST

"But wait," I seem to hear you protesting. "All characters don't have the same importance in a story. They don't all fulfill the same story function. The secondary player doesn't merit as much attention as my lead female."

So what does the fiction writer do about that? She evaluates the importance of each planned character in the story to be written, and then she lavishes most attention and thought on the most important ones. This means identifying each character's role in the story, and how important it is.

We can do this by working with the same character cards we've been using, looking at them in a slightly different way and adding a line or two, perhaps, to some of them.

So take out the cards you have accumulated on some character and make sure that you already have—or can now supply—the following minimum information:

1. Character's name, age and brief (!) factual biography.

2. Character's dominant impression and major tags.

3. Character's goal, problem or lacking that motivates him in this story.

4. The action, event or setting that introduces this character into the story.

5. The action, event or place where we will leave this character at the conclusion of his part in the story.

6. A brief physical description that will help identify the character, but which may have nothing to do with tags—such things as height or weight or hair color, for example.

This work might spark your imagination. If so, follow that spark to the point where it loses its usefulness. What is that point? Probably past a page or two; I've known writers who became so enamored of a character at this point that they churned out twenty to thirty pages of static character description — far more than they could ever use in a short story. After such an emotionally draining experience, they never finished the story planned for that character.

Even if you severely control what you imagine about your character at this point, you may be amazed by how much you now know. Several characters, in fact, may start to seem equally fascinating and strong. This can become confusing. What do you do about that? You now rank your characters in terms of story importance.

Here's how.

You have already ranked your characters in chapter eight, when you decided some would be major and others secondary. We have also taken a look at story viewpoint, and you realize that the most important character in your story will be your viewpoint character. Thus you already have done much of the work necessary to rank your story people. So let's just take it a step further.

We have seen that the viewpoint character is the most important person in your story — the one through whose senses, thoughts and feelings we will experience the tale. Each of us lives his life in a single viewpoint, so a story told from a single viewpoint will tend to be the most lifelike and convincing for the reader. This character's goal or problem will be at the center of the story, and his fate will most worry the reader. Therefore, this character deserves the most planning attention of all. Call him hero or protagonist, but make sure you have given maximum thought and feeling to planning his personality.

As stated earlier, in most fiction the second-most important character will be the one who struggles against the hero, or makes life complicated for him. In a story of conflict, this antagonist or villain would fight actively against the hero. In a story of discovery or decision, he would muddy the waters or work to make the hero decide the wrong thing — or not discover something vital. If your story is about romance or intense friendship, this hierarchy may be changed. The villain or antagonist could become the third-most important character, as you dwell lovingly on every aspect of the supportive relationship between viewpoint character and friend or lover.

Beyond this point, ranking your characters can be pretty murky business. Often you will have a very important love interest who ranks third behind the antagonist. Other times you may have a character who functions as a vital *confidante*, to whom the viewpoint character tells his innermost thoughts, fears and desires. You may decide that someone fulfilling one of these story roles is so important that he merits major planning attention.

In a mystery, you may have a suspect or even a false suspect— a red-herring character designed to confuse the reader and throw suspicion away from the real culprit. Such a character may assume serious proportions. Similarly, you have a complicating person, someone who is neither a villain nor a suspect, but whose presence messes up the neatness of the viewpoint character's life in unexpected ways.

You may even have a character primarily designed to be *a foil*. Such a character is in the story mainly to provide contrast with someone else. In the crudest terms, this is why so many classic comic teams of years past featured a short, fat guy and a tall, skinny guy, or an idiot and someone a lot smarter (Abbott and Costello, for one example, or Martin and Lewis, for another). Standing such characters next to one another tends to make each seem more vivid because of the contrast between them.

In short fiction, however, you will seldom find a pure foil character. If you believe you need one in your story, you should look for ways to add this function to another character already designated as a more important role-player.

At any rate, you should give considerable thought to identifying the role of each character planned for your story and ranking the importance of each. For the major ones, you need to do as much planning as possible. For lesser ones, a single trait and tag may be sufficient. This is a decision you have to make, and it's important not only to save unnecessary work: If you ineptly provide loving attention to a very minor character in your story, the reader will be confused; she will assume that the character is to be important (or why would the author spend so much effort on him?), and then she is baffled when the implied promise of prominence does not pan out.

This planning work will inevitably pay off in another way, too. It will surely clarify your thinking about character interactions— which is to say, your plot.

## FINDING THE SELF-CONCEPT

There is, however, an additional step the professional writer should take in defining major characters. This step is associated with the *life script* that we discussed in the second Time Out section. You will need another card for each story person whose personality is to be further amplified.

On a fresh card for your protagonist, for example, here is what you do: Write *I am:* as a verbal statement by that character, as if he or she were speaking. Then complete the statement in twenty words or less, having the character state his or her self-definition.

For example, many persons in real life or fiction tend to identify themselves by their job or major role in life. So one character might complete the statement by saying, *I am: an excellent surgeon.* While you might get deep into another character's heart and have her write, *I am: a single mother, a very lonely person.*

Other real people—and characters—might define themselves by a more general description, such as, *I am: a person who tries hard but never quite succeeds.* Or, *I am: a generally happy person who usually gets whatever she sets out after.*

A very few might define themselves more generally still, and perhaps very meaningfully, like the man in one of my classes who wrote for his self-definition, *I am: a failure in life.* Far happier was the time when a woman read her self-definition card, saying, *I am: a child of God.* What a terribly sad self-definition in one instance, and what a wonderful one in the other.

The point of this exercise lies in the theory that humans live by—and cling to—a *self-concept.* We are, says S.I. Hayakawa in his book *Symbol, Status and Personality,* "a symbolic class of life." We come up with a self-concept, then work like the devil to live up to (or down to!) that self-concept.

To put this another way, our primary goal in life is not preservation of the self, but preservation of the symbolic self. We will risk death to retain our symbolic image of ourselves. Why else, for example, would a soldier throw himself on a live grenade, assuring his own death, to save the lives of virtual strangers standing nearby? On a less serious note, why would a man who sees himself as a sportsman spend hundreds of dollars every year on fishing tackle to catch six dollars worth of fish? Why—to carry the example one step further—do some people sign up for ruinous monthly payments for an automobile far more expensive than they can really afford, unless having that big car somehow enhances and reinforces their self-concept? Why must one person live in a grand house while someone else, with the same income, can be as cozy as a bug in something far more modest? Why, even, do some people work themselves literally to death, while others always seem to have time to play? Why are some people happy and others always sad?

In all these cases, and many others that might be cited as examples, the central truth is that we form a self-concept or, to use the transactional analysis term, a *life script*. We live and act and feel and think and surround ourselves with objects to maintain our most precious possession, that self-concept. Notice how often you hear people define themselves in the most casual conversation. "I didn't go on vacation because I'm in love with my job, and that's just the kind of person I am," someone may tell you. Or, "I wouldn't go out with him because I know what he wants, and I'm not that kind of girl." Or, "I'm a lover, not a fighter." And so on.

What this further demonstrates is the fact that we not only live by our self-concept, but the self-concept is the belief about one's essential nature *that is admissable to consciousness*. Thus you don't get into murky Freudian waters in determining the self-concept of a story character. Knowing what you already know about such character, you can put yourself into her viewpoint and have her state how she defines herself.

Once you have thought about this matter, you will see why an additional card should be filled out for every major character, having the character define herself. Everything else about the character will be affected by this statement of self-definition.

Just as an exercise to check your understanding of the matter, please grab another blank card right now and label it "activities and possessions." Then, on the next line of the card, have your character say, "I am a dedicated outdoorsman." Now use the rest of the card to list several activities a character with such a self-concept would engage in, and several possessions such a character would like own.

Take time to do this now, before proceeding, and I'll do the same. It's an easy one and shouldn't take long.

◆ ◆ ◆

Finished? Good. So am I.

On my card I jotted, *Camping; hunting; fishing; back-packing.* Then, following the same line of reasoning, I wrote for possessions,

*Tent, fishing gear, Jeep, rifles, elk antler trophy over fireplace in family den.*

Even starting with the same self-concept—a dedicated outdoorsman—you probably came up with a vastly different list. Perhaps you thought of a tropical clime for your character, and listed things like scuba diving and walking on the beach. Or perhaps your outdoors-person played golf or rode bikes in the Olympics.

You see, determining a self-concept for a character in no way limits the means by which you can show that self-concept in story action. Your "outdoorsman" will not be mine. So every character can be unique and independent. But in every case the character will be internally consistent with his self-concept—and by knowing this you can further develop a character who is interesting and believeable.

## SUMMARY

Ranking your story characters and determining the role each will play in the story is a great help in deciding which characters may demand additional characterization work. For the majors, a tag for a given trait will not be enough; you need to devise tag clusters, and wave them often.

Additional cards almost certainly will have to be filled out for your most important story people.

An understanding of the importance of the self-concept will help you further define your character as the character sees himself. Then you can devise additional interesting—and convincing—aspects surrounding that character to show the self-concept and make the character more credible and vivid.

Whatever additional cards need to be made for major characters, they should be filled out now, before you proceed to the next chapter. For we are almost to the point where we meld all the planning into a cohesive map for your next short story.

*Chapter Eleven*

# Planning Your Route and Drawing Your Map

PROGRESS CHECK:

✔ *Have you completed work on the self-concept of all major characters?*

✔ *Does work continue on any needed factual research?*

✔ *Are you still observing real-life people and making notes on them?*

✔ *What observations—about others' work or your own—have you entered lately in your journal?*

H ere we talk in more detail about plot.

When you read a story and find yourself gripped by its movement and suspense, you can be sure that the writer did some good structural planning—set up strong plot architecture to hold everything together and draw the desired emotional responses from the reader at the desired times.

But what *is* plotting? And how can you build the most effective plot for the story you're now planning and nearly ready to write?

First, let's do away with a common misunderstanding. Plot is *not* a rigid framework, a kind of pre-ordained pattern in which you fill in the blanks. Plot is not the same for every story. Plot is not "formula."

Plot is dynamic. It's a way of seeing your material and structuring your storytelling so that it will capture the reader's attention early and hold it to the very end. It's a form of storytelling that keeps the reader involved and guessing, and lets him finish the yarn with a sense of satisfaction and dramatic fulfillment.

Plot is, in other words, not a format. It is a process.

Whether you were fully aware of it, you've already done quite a lot of preliminary work on your plotting as you worked through the map to this point. For example, when you made major decisions about your story people in chapter ten, you automatically began to make assumptions about story locale, the kind of problem such characters might deal with, some of the action and even the ending. Similarly, when you decided who the viewpoint character was to be, you limited the action you could describe, and probably began to see the viewpointed action with some kind of emotional coloration.

In your continuing factual research for the story, you have also inadvertently limited plot possibilities. This is not a bad thing, because it clarifies your vision of the possible story. For example, if you have been researching a modern hospital environment—interviewing doctors and nurses and the like—you have pretty clearly eliminated a plot involving big game hunting, a trip to the moon or a murder trial. And in limiting decisions of this nature, you have begun to make crucial plot decisions such as the time length of the story, roughly the number of pages the telling is likely to require, its pace, its dependence on action or dialogue or introspections, and much more.

Now, however, it's time to move forward.

## FINDING THE STORY QUESTION

You may already know the answer to this question, or it might be one you need to ponder further at this time: What do you want the reader of your story to worry about?

In every story, one reader worry is stronger than any others that might occur. This dominant worry is called *the story question*.

Have you determined what your story question is to be?

The question is related to character goal, reader worry along the way, and how the story is to turn out. The beginning of the story should clearly tell the reader what the goal or problem is (so she can start to worry); the middle of the story should deal with incidents relating to this worry; and the end of the story must relax the worry or tension.

To put this another way, the story starts with a question, the plot revolves around attempts to find an answer to the question, and the ending *answers* the question.

The story question can be virtually anything that goes to the character's self-concept and desire for happiness. For example, any of the following might be a legitimate story question:

- Will David get the better job he is seeking?
- Can Max climb the mountain?
- Do Phil and Mary ever work out their disagreement?

- Can Jennifer shake the feeling of impending doom?
- Can Ted learn who killed Adam Jones?
- Will Martha find a way to stop feeling so adrift?
- Will Helen find something horrible behind the locked door?
- Can Alice learn why that eerie blue light shines from a window?
- Will Ralph win reconciliation with his embittered father?

This seems a baffling variety of possibilities—and that's good, because it shows you can build a story question out of just about any story situation. But you should also note that these questions also have something in common. *All can be answered!*

None is particularly abstract or philosphical, although abstract ideas and personal philosophies may lie behind the value structure inherent in any of them. In the story question about Ted seeking a killer, for example, there might lurk a strong statement about friendship, loyalty and persistence. But the question itself is not so amorphous. The reader wants to know what to worry about, and she wants the story ending to provide an answer to the question— and nothing less will do.

Thus you must plot your story in such a way as to introduce not only a character in a setting, and not even just a problem. You must also plant the story question in your reader's mind. It must be clear and specific and answerable.

Similarly, the body of the plot must relate in some way to this story question. You can't ask a question about climbing a mountain, for example, and then let your plot wander into discussions of raising orchids, or whether the new fertilizer will help them bloom.

And at the end of the story, you have to answer the question as asked. Given a question like the first one listed above, you can't stick on an ending that says something like, "Well, I don't know if he ever got a better job, but he started seeing a psychiatrist." Or, "I'm not telling you about the quest for a job, but David did meet a nice girl."

You can't cheat your readers on this point. Play fair. Anything less than a just answer, and the reader will throw your story against the nearest wall.

A clear knowledge of the story question will assure you of a more satisfying story. It will also assure unity and cohesion. This matter is so important you need to work on it before going on. Do something to make sure the story question is clear in your own mind.

To do this, we again use a card. On the card, write down the story question in a few words. Make sure it *is* a question, and that it's the kind of action question for which you can provide an answer.

Then, on the same card, write the answer. Make sure it directly answers the question you just defined.

If you have never dealt much with story question before—or if you have many unrelated plot incidents and characters floating around in your mind—this story-question process may be difficult, and take some time. Keep working on it until you feel confident that you have defined both question and answer as clearly and specifically as possible.

Remember that a vague story question leaves you no anchor for development of your plot. And a vague answer at the end of the story will doom it to reader dissatisfaction—and failure.

Once you feel sure you have written the question and the answer as succinctly as possible, get out two more fresh cards. On one, print the story question. On the second, print the answer. Then tack or tape these two cards on the wall over your word processor! They form the basis for everything else you do about plotting.

## THE STRUCTURE BEHIND GOOD PLOT

Of course a pretty enormous question remains for the storyteller, even after defining the story question (point A) and the answer (point B).

That is: How do you get from A to B in the most effective way?

The answer lies at the heart of plotting, that dynamic process by which the writer provides a structure designed to keep the story developing on-track, while at the same time fascinating the reader.

Here's the trick, stated as simply as possible: you get from A to B by building a series of *scenes*. The scenes are then linked logically and emotionally by *sequels*.

What are scenes and sequels? I've written a book on this subject, *Scene and Structure*, available from Writer's Digest Books. For our purposes here, I'll give you a condensed look at the subject.

In its simplest form, the scene is a structural component, a brief bit of story action played out in the story "now," onstage, and presented moment by moment. It is the actors onstage before the reader's eyes, in struggle over progress toward reaching an answer to the story question. Its appeal lies in its immediacy and the conflict or difficulty it portrays. The scene has a definite form, which we'll get to in a minute.

The sequel, also in its simplest definition, is a structural component that provides a condensed record of how your character gets from one scene to the next. It presents a character's feelings and thoughts as he plans his next move in his ongoing struggle to find an answer to the story question. The sequel, too, has a definite form.

## Scenes

Scenes have outcomes that plunge your viewpoint character into longer or shorter sequels, and sequels then result in the character moving into another scene after emotion and thought. Sometimes scenes appear quiet and sometimes highly dramatic; in any case, they are characterized by some kind of *conflict*.

The result of one scene may be another so immediate and obvious that a sequel need not be "played" for the reader—as when, for example, a melodramatic physical fight ends with the viewpoint character being thrown into a rushing river: here it's so obvious that he now has a new goal (to save himself from drowning) and a new opponent (the river itself). In virtually all circumstances, however, it helps the writer to imagine what the sequel would be like if it *were* played—what feelings and thoughts the character must be experiencing, no matter how obvious the new decision, or how intense the time pressure that may prevent the scene from being presented to the reader.

A short story may contain only one or two scenes, while a novel may contain hundreds. In an action story, scenes may rush one after another with little story time for character reflection. In a thoughtful story, scenes may be rather slight and the author may devote herself to lengthy sequels minutely examining character emotion and thought.

Thus the kind of story you like to write can determine whether you plan long scenes and short sequels or vice versa. That's another reason I urged you earlier to think hard about the kind of story you planned to write. The kind of story you want to produce will tend to determine its plot structure.

Every scene centers on some rather immediate goal that the viewpoint character feels compelled to reach *right now*. This goal or problem must be stated as clearly as possible so the reader sees where the character is trying to go. Once the reader sees what the character is after, the reader will turn the stated scene goal into a *scene question*, and worry about that while the scene plays out. So just as suspense is generated by story question, the bits of the story called scenes are carried along by reader curiosity about the scene question.

Once the scene question has been shown as clearly as possible — often by having the viewpoint character simply think or even state aloud what it is — then further development depends on some sort of struggle taking place. It's somewhat obvious that if the character (a) has a long-term goal, and (b) believes achievement of a scene goal will get her much closer to that long-term goal, and (c) easily and quickly achieves the scene goal, that character is fat and happy and moving right along, thank you — and the reader relaxes, and there went your story tension.

To keep your reader tense, you can't have easy, casual stuff going on after the goal is stated. Thus the struggle that forms the bulk of the scene. Usually this occurs between the protagonist and the antagonist, although sometimes the fight can be entirely inside the character's head and heart as warring impulses rage.

I prefer outside struggle — conflict — between characters. It's far more dramatic and easy for the reader to follow and get involved in. Also, ending the scene is usually easier if a real fight has been going on.

How does the scene end? As with a story ending, you end a scene by answering the question that was posed at the outset. So just as there is a story question (and your story ending has to answer it), there is always a scene question — and the end of the scene must answer that.

This scene-ending answer, unless it falls at the very end of your story, ordinarily should be some form of setback or bad news for your main character. At best, on a few occasions, the answer can provide a partial or severely limited bit of progress, but nothing delightful. Why? Because, if everything in the scene turns out swimmingly, the character is fat and happy again — and you've lost the reader's interest.

Furthermore, if you show a character just bumbling along and having a lot of good fortune, the reader usually won't develop a strong feeling about him. But if you show the same character fighting, getting knocked back, then regrouping and fighting again, the reader will admire the character and care about him.

In short, bad fortune for the character at the end of the scene is usually wonderful for the author working to build sympathy and suspense.

So let's suppose you've just designed a scene in which the character wants to achieve something right now, as a step toward attainment of the story goal. Then suppose you have introduced sharp conflict with another character who stands in opposition to the hero's story goal. And at the end, in a disastrous turn of events, the hero has lost his immediate goal.

Wonderful!

But how do you get him to another scene?

## Sequels

Sometimes, as stated above, the next step is so obvious or the situation so intense and pressure-filled that the character has no time (or you the author have no need) to provide a linking sequel. More often, however, you need to show the character's emotional reaction, his thoughts and his new decision—which will lead him into the next scene.

To make the distinction clear, let's restate it. The classic pattern of a scene, as we just implied, is goal . . . conflict . . . disaster. The classic pattern of the sequel is emotion . . . thought . . . decision.

How much space will you devote to telling how the character feels, or how long he thinks about options for further action? The answer depends on the kind of story you're telling and the kind of writer you are. If you're writing a painful psychological story, and you happen to be the kind of writer who loves to define emotions and thoughts, you may write very long sequels indeed. If you're writing a traditional western, on the other hand, and do best with action, your sequel may be no longer than having the hero fall off his horse and draw his shooting iron.

Long scenes and little sequels will tend to make a fast-moving story. Short scenes and long sequels will tend to make a slow-moving one. The big-scene story depends on action. The big-sequel story depends on thought and emotion.

Whatever kind of story you plan to write, however, and whatever kind of writer you tend to be, I think you will find it much easier to plan a cohesive, logical, compelling story if you plan every possible scene and sequel as if you intended to present every one in all detail.

Therefore, clearly your next step in planning the story you are about to tell will involve planning all your scenes and sequels. You'll do this with more planning cards, in this case scene and sequel cards.

## PLANNING THE SCENES AND SEQUELS

On the top of a blank card, write *Scene 1*. On the next line, write *Viewpoint*, and fill in the name of the character who will provide the viewpoint in this, the first scene of the story.

On the next line of the same card, write *Goal*. Then put down, in ten words or less, what your viewpoint character wants to accomplish in this scene.

On the next line of the same card, write *Problem*. Then describe, as briefly as possible, the major complication. A great many times it will be the antagonist or some other character fighting actively against the hero, trying to make sure he doesn't reach the scene goal. Other times—less often—it may be something far more abstract, such as a storm or even character confusion.

On the next line of your card, write the word *Conflict*. In a few words, sketch how the antagonist (or storm, or whatever) dynamically stands between the viewpoint character and the immediate scene goal. You may sketch in six to eight steps in the conflict, using words like "Tom won't open office . . . then opens it but won't provide papers . . . then argues papers are privileged . . . tries to foist off wrong papers on hero . . . tells other lies."

Finally—perhaps on the back of the card if you have run out of space—write the word *Disaster*. Then in ten words or less sketch in what awful twist takes place at the end of the scene to put the viewpoint character farther behind the eight ball than he was at the beginning.

A few words of additional explanation: Note that I asked you to write down the character's goal in ten words or less. This was not simply for brevity, but because you need to clarify and boil down every scene goal to its core; this will help you keep on track when you write the scene, for this goal is what the struggle is about.

Note, too, if you will, the words "this specific scene" in the paragraph that followed. It's important to remember that the immediate goal in *this* scene should somehow be different from the one that may follow it. Otherwise, if you keep writing scenes about almost exactly the same goal, the reader will begin to get a weary "here-we-go-again" feeling. Also, the scene goal must not simply be the story goal. Remember that each scene is a stepping stone toward the story goal—a move toward the ultimate goal, the viewpoint character hopes.

You may also wish to pause a moment and think about the advice about filling in a twist after the word "disaster." Remember that the disaster must grow logically but unexpectedly out of the conflict that just took place. (You can't satisfy the reader, for example, by having Joe and Tom argue about the papers, then have someone run in and say Joe's mother just died; that's a freak of fate that has nothing to do with what's been going on.) To put this another way, the disaster must grow out of the effort that just took place, so we get a sense of the character having tried, and paradoxically, as a result, finds himself in worse trouble than if he had done nothing.

This organic growth of the disaster directly out of the conflict accomplishes several things. Perhaps most important, it keeps the story moving in a straight, logical (but unanticipated) line. For another, it tends to create both admiration for the try-again viewpoint character, as well as sympathy for him.

Having completed this scene card, at least for the moment, you probably have a general idea of what at least some of the subsequent scenes are going to be about. Using a fresh card for each, you should repeat the planning process outlined above. You may wish to pause in your reading at this point, and go ahead and do that considerable—and vitally important—work.

◆ ◆ ◆

Once you've planned and mapped as many scenes as you can see at this point, the next step is to plan your sequels.

What you need to do, in effect, is create a sequel card to go between each pair of scene cards, so that your story-planning pattern becomes scene-sequel . . . scene-sequel . . . scene-sequel, up to the climax of the story.

You may not write every sequel, as noted earlier in this chapter. But knowing how every one of them would go, if written, will help you with logic and character emotion.

So let's take another fresh card and write atop it *Sequel 1*.

Having done that, write the word *Feelings* on a new line. Then, in ten words or so, sketch the uppermost emotions you imagine would go through your character's mind as a result of the disaster that just took place in the preceding scene.

Having done this, on a new line write the word *Thoughts*. Briefly express the kinds of thoughts — and possible new actions — the character might go through after working through her first feelings of shock or fear or rage.

On another new line, write the word *Decision*. And after it fill in the active decision the character should make to get her to the goal that will open the next scene, following on the next scene card.

Note, please, that when the character is thinking, he may be confused and consider many story options. But as he works through rejections and finally nears his next planned action, *he is plotting the progress of your story*. In this way, I seldom find myself thinking, "What will I have happen next?" Instead, I get into the mind of my viewpoint character, and let him or her make the decision in my imagination. (All I have to do is make sure it isn't a decision that would ruin my long-term plans for the story!)

Also, when you fill in the "Decision" line, remember that this should be some new course of action, toward some new subsidiary goal, which — when the hero starts after it and meets new opposition — will be the stuff of your second scene card. Be sure to fill out a sequel card to put between all the scenes, linking them dynamically.

If you have never planned a story in scenes and sequels, you may have an awful time filling out some of these cards. Crumpled cards may litter your office floor; you may lose patience with the process or with yourself; you may get stuck here and there.

Keep at it! This is your building material for your story map. All the planning done now, painful as it may get, is preferable to an accidental story, or an unbelievable one, or — worst of all — one you get stuck on and never finish.

At some point, perhaps after a struggle, you will indeed have all your cards made out in sequence up to the climax. You may not be perfectly happy with all of them, but you can always hope to revise later. The most important point is to have all the parts of the story laid out in order, even if you don't like some of the details.

Take your time and do this work now.

## TESTING YOUR SCENE AND SEQUEL CARDS

What's the next step?

Before leaving this planning phase of your scenes and sequels, it's time to step back a bit and consider the kind of story your cards delineate.

First, you should give some thought to the length of story your cards predict. You may not be entirely accurate in your estimate, but obviously you'll have a story that's too long if you find that you have thirty or forty scene cards! By the same token, if you would really like to write a 10,000-word story, two or three scene cards may not be enough.

If you find you have planned far too many scenes and sequels for the length you hope to achieve, it's time to study your cards and pull out a few, starting the story later in the action, perhaps, or eliminating a secondary character, or cutting in the middle somewhere. Your study of desired markets may help you decide on a length.

You should also consider the kind of story you have been hoping to tell. You'll remember that big scenes and little sequels tend to make for a fast-moving story. This kind of speed is proper for an action story, suspense or adventure. It might be entirely wrong if you plan to write a love story or psychological study, in which scant action (few big scenes) and heavy feeling and thought (big sequels) would achieve the desired effect and also produce a much slower-moving story.

Again, you may feel uneasy with trying to make some of these preliminary decisions. We'll be refining them in the next chapter. But in the meantime you should take heart from the knowledge that you can always revise anything, anytime and work done now is superior to blank confusion, even if you have to make changes later.

As before, I can't stress too heavily the importance of doing this work *now*, before moving ahead. We have reached the crucial turning point for many would-be short story writers. The ones doomed to fail will skip ahead impatiently and not take enough time to do all this work just as well as possible. Those likely to succeed as writers will be patient and thoughtful and take as much time as necessary to do this right.

## CHECKING YOUR WORK BEFORE MOVING ON

On your worktable, or a floor not likely to be disturbed by intruders, lay out your scene and sequel cards in sequence, two or three rows — scene-sequel, scene-sequel. What you will come up with will look a little like a block diagram. At this point, however, the block diagram is made up of cards that can be moved around.

Examine the pattern your cards form. Do they follow logically?

Is the timing in the right order? Does every scene relate somehow to the story question? Does each sequel grow out of the scene that preceded it . . . and lead to the next scene? Are there scenes you might pull out without truly harming your story's impact? Is there a clear goal in each scene? Conflict? A disaster? In each sequel, are the character's feelings and thoughts believable? Have you forgotten anything?

You may find that you will move some cards around—pull one, replace another, perhaps change the order. That's fine. That's the beauty of the card system. You can stand back, examine what you plan, and improve it piecemeal.

This checking of your work, and reevaluation, may take some time. I would urge you to leave your cards in place for two or three days even after you feel confident you have them all set up as well as possible; having the cards arrayed before you will stimulate both your conscious and unconscious mind to ponder the structure and plan even when you are in another room, presumably doing something else.

During this interval of a few days you may find yourself preoccupied with the card contents and pattern, and that's good. Your spouse or friend might even come in sometime and find you staring moodily at your card "block diagram." They may ask you what you're doing.

You can say mysteriously, "I'm plotting." Chances are they won't have the slightest idea what you mean.

## SUMMARY

Stories are structured with scenes and sequels. Planning these in advance is really what is meant by planning. You should write out a card for every scene and sequel planned for your story, and arrange them in the order you plan to present them in the story. This is vital work.

# THE BEAUTY – AND
# UTILITY – OF SACRIFICE

B y now you're deep into the final planning of your story. It could be that all your preparation has left you with uncertainty in some key part of your story – what you might do to make your reader like your character more, for example, or how to show which of two characters is most admirable. If you haven't yet worked out every detail about the ending, you may be thinking hard about the best way to end the story.

A few brief thoughts about sacrifice may help you see things from a different perspective. A new perspective, in turn, could help you get over any problems you may be experiencing with your late-stage planning.

"Sacrifice" might mean different things to different people. Here, however, we're looking at what might be termed *self*-sacrifice, and for a laudable goal or cause.

To phrase this differently, when the word "sacrifice" is used here, we mean sacrifice of one's self for a principle.

Sounds a little grim. Didn't people like Joan of Arc sacrifice themselves for a principle? And look how she ended up. Didn't Galileo go through some personal hell because he sacrificed himself rather than recant his scientific observations? Can you think of other cases where a person stuck to his guns – and paid most dearly for it?

Of course. And this may be exactly the point. Sacrifice of this kind carries with it extremely high risk; when one stands up for a goal or belief, whatever the consequences, the consequences may be terrible indeed.

But it is precisely this kind of behavior that makes most of us deeply admire another human being. Nothing, it seems, ennobles a person like the demonstrated willingness to sacrifice everything for principle. We sympathize with a person willing to risk this kind of self-sacrifice; we root for them and even love them, and we certainly care about their fate.

It follows, then, that a splendid way to create a sympathetic and admirable character in a short story is to set up one or more situations in which the character faces a choice between a selfish momentary gain and likely terrible suffering . . . between principle and expediency . . . between selfishness and selflessness.

It has often been said that the one characteristic that separates "good" or admirable characters from the "bad" or hateful ones is ruthlessness. Both antagonist and protagonist may begin a story saying they will do anything to reach a goal. But as the story puts them into conflict or confusion over a goal, we begin to see that only one of the major characters really *is* willing to do *anything* to win out. This is the epitome of selfishness, recklessness and cruelty; because of his ruthlessness, this story-person loses our sympathy, is disliked, and becomes the antagonist or "villain."

The other major character may encounter a number of situations in the adventure when he can seemingly gain a temporary but significant advantage simply by doing something ruthless too. But *this* character has some principles. There are things he simply cannot do because they are so far out of his moral and ethical universe. He "has ruth." He is willing to sacrifice his own struggle—himself—for principle.

We like this character. We root for him. We care increasingly about how things will turn out for him.

The lesson is clear. One way to keep a story on the boil, while at the same time sorting out the sympathetic characters from the evil ones, is to use sacrifice—to set up story situations wherein the hero sacrifices and the villain does not.

At first thought this might seem artificial and contrived to you. But if you think about it a while, you may begin to see that sacrifice comes in all shapes and sizes, and often it is just as easy to emphasize a tinge of sacrifice in a story development as it is to ignore the opportunity.

Good writers very often take advantage of almost every plot twist to give it a semblance of choice or decision-challenge for the viewpoint character. These may be quite minor but can still be effective.

Thus, instead of having your hero drive to the corner to pick up her friend for a trip to the grocery (nice enough, and a tag for kindness), you might just as easily give the hero a slight cold and headache, and then have someone else in the story say, "You really shouldn't go out today; you might make yourself really sick." *Then* if she goes ahead with the trip, her action is mildly sacrificial. We like her better as a result.

Such simple additions or modifications to your existing plot developments may make a difference in reader sympathy for a character. Of course this technique, like many others, can be carried to an extreme, making the character appear almost saintlike. But the insertion of small, almost reflexive sacrificial decisions by a character — along with a few more significant ones, perhaps — generally builds a character in a desirable way. I would suggest putting in plenty of such decisions as they occur to you. If you later decide you might have overdone it a bit, you can always tone down or remove a few such decisions during the revision process. Better to have something like this in the story, and tone it down later, than to ignore its possibilities altogether; it's almost always easier to delete or change on revision than to insert some brand-new element.

## SACRIFICE AND CONFLICT

More dramatic than the illustration above, and also often already in your story by implication, is the more dramatic kind of choice that grows out of serious conflict. Suppose, for example, you now have a situation in your story in which Sammy interviews for a new job, but doesn't get it. All well and good: It's easy to see how this could develop into a scene in which Sammy enters asking for the job, experiences conflict or dialogue at cross-purposes with an interviewer, and then is shocked to learn that he was considered too pushy during the interview, and so now faces the disaster of walking out on the street with no chance at the job, or any other with that company.

Why not consider adding the sacrifice element? What if, in addition to everything outlined just above, the interviewer mentions two or three times that the winning applicant must be willing to do anything to outdo the representative of Acme Corp., the rival firm. What if the interviewer finally asks point-blank: "Will you help us spread the story that Acme's product line faces a recall soon?" What if our hero knows for a fact that Acme products are sound?

*Now* we have set something up where we can still have a disaster at the end, but now our hero brings it on himself because he sees that his best chance of landing the job is to say he'll be unethical; but he can't go that far, as badly as he needs the job; so he sacrifices, or at least risks great loss through sacrifice, by telling the interviewer that, sorry, he can't go out and lie about a competitor's product line.

And sure enough, as a result he walks out jobless, the interviewer's angry words ("Don't ever come back, you wimp!") echoing in his ears.

The result of adding the element of sacrifice to a scene plan that was already workable: greater admiration for the character, increased reader tension, more suspense, a more readable story.

All story scenes or incidents can't be turned around like the ones shown here, of course. But time and again I have seen young writers overlook incredibly powerful possibilities for sacrifice in their stories. While you may not always come up with a sacrifice angle in the development of your story, or might sometimes choose not to follow up on a possibility after thinking of it, you should always be alert to the multifaceted power of sacrifice, big or small, and how you might use such sacrifice in the next segment of your story simply by adding one small "what if?"

The sacrifice may be very slight, such as the woman deciding to risk a worse cold. Or it might be much more serious, like Sammy in the example just above. Some writers sprinkle the most incidental, minor sacrifices through their stories like pepper on an egg. Some writers use sacrifice only at major turning points in the story. You can—and should—consider both. It might help you in the exact spot where you now feel a bit stuck in your planning.

## SACRIFICIAL DECISION AT THE CLIMAX

However much you elect to use sacrifice in the development of your character's progress through the story, a most powerful potential exists for attempting to add an angle of sacrifice—sacrificial decision—at the story's climax.

How does this work?

Remember that your story has raised a story question of some kind. At some level of intensity, the story has developed around progress (or lack of progress) toward discovery of some kind of answer to that story question. Remember, too, that almost always, even in the quietest stories, someone wants, yearns, wishes for a conclusion, some kind of answer.

If you use sacrifice as part of your story's conclusion, you will devise a climax scene in which the answer to the story question finally must be answered, for good or ill. You will set up a final dramatic confrontation or a final tense introspection or something else in which no more delay is possible, and the question must be answered *now*.

If you use sacrifice at this point in the setting-up, you will devise a way to make the answer to the story question somehow devolve on a choice to be made by the viewpoint character. And you will give this choice a strong element of possible sacrifice.

Consider, for example, the Biblical story of Abraham, ordered by his God to take his only son Isaac up to the mountaintop and there slay him as proof of his love of God. Abraham is faced with the ultimate moral dilemma, a choice between love of his only son and love of his God. Everything in Abraham's life comes down to this. He must make a decision, and now.

This is powerful stuff. It comes out of the same operational foundation of fiction that lies behind Pip's endless acts of selflessness — and the selfish choices made by evil people — in *Great Expectations*. It shares the sacrificial decision machinery of sailors who must finally decide whether to risk all and face charges of mutiny in *The Caine Mutiny*. It's the same device used in so many classic short stories, often those of Poe, whose character makes the wrong or selfish choice — and pays horribly as a result.

If you can find a way to set up the climax of your story so that it includes a clear choice involving sacrificial decision, you will find the most powerful way to conclude the story, at the same time most clearly confronting whatever ethical questions lay behind the story as theme in the first place. When writers say their theme will emerge as an inevitable dynamic of how fiction works, they're talking about this kind of potent relationship between what you have happen and what it *means*. If sacrifice — and argument over — principle is involved, the theme simply must come out as a basis for whatever decision the protagonist makes.

Note something else about the use of sacrifice in the climax of your story. If you elect to have your protagonist make a decision in favor of principle, even expecting to lose everything as a result, then you must do two further things to satisfy the reader.

Remember that the act of sacrifice powerfully moved the reader to admire and even love the character. In most cases, it's not wise to show the character making the sacrificial decision, then end your story by making him suffer horribly for it. This means that in most cases you need to contrive a situation in which the sacrificial character expects to lose, makes the moral decision anyway, and then paradoxically wins, or at least finds solace.

This doesn't sound easy, and it's even harder than it sounds, unless you want to cheat and just have the cavalry come to the rescue. Far better if you have tucked away in the elements of the climactic decision a hidden way out for the character—a possible twist that leaves the reader saying, "Good lord! Of course! It was there all the time!"

Remember the story of Abraham. He decided to sacrifice Isaac, and raised the knife. He made a decision to sacrifice all. How could he possibly win? God stayed his hand, and said in effect that this had been only a test.

And we, as readers of the story, experience intense relief along with a strong sense of paradoxical insight. We realize that Abraham would never have had peace again if he had denied his God. Now he has both his God and his son; he has been tested and has emerged victorious.

Entire books have been based largely on the idea of sacrifice in drama and fiction. One such is *The Basic Formulas of Fiction* by William Foster-Harris (University of Oklahoma Press). You may wish to enquire further into such a book.

For our purposes here, the discussion as given seems adequate. It has even carried with it a certain element of risk. The danger? That you might become so enamored of the machinery of sacrifice that you start making *every* scene involve sacrifice . . . that you twist the ending of *every* story to accommodate sacrifice.

That would be a disaster for you. Remain aware of the power of sacrifice, as a character-builder during the progress of your story and as an ultimate test at the climax. If you give some thought to taking advantage of the dynamism several times in a story, or at the climax, that's fine. But if this particular story does not seem the type that lends itself to constant or climax sacrifice, don't force the mechanism onto this story.

Awareness and consideration of sacrifice, in other words, is sufficient. When you can use it, use it. When you can't, don't inflict in on a story where it doesn't fit. But *do* keep it in mind! Your characters may thank you for it.

## Chapter Twelve

# Fine-Tuning the Plan

---

PROGRESS CHECK:

✔ *Are all your scene and sequel cards ready and in order?*

✔ *Have you allowed a few days' thought time about your story pattern?*

✔ *Have you virtually completed any needed research?*

---

I t may be that you have made several intuitive jumps ahead of me, and are already hard at work on your first draft. That's fine. However, before I *urge* you to start writing the first draft of your manuscript, there are a couple of final fine-tuning steps you may wish to take.

These have to do with integrating your earlier work with the scene-sequel planning, and looking ahead to make sure the story heads toward exactly the kind of ending you desire.

## MELDING YOUR EARLIER WORK INTO THE STRUCTURAL PLAN

In the last chapter you laid out the pattern of your story with scene-sequel cards. Now, possibly your earlier work on characters and setting was so clear in your mind that melding these aspects of story into the scene-sequel card layout came almost automatically. However, it won't hurt to make sure all the previous planning is dovetailed with the structural plan—the nearly finished short story map.

To make sure everything is together at this point, let me suggest the following procedure while your scene-sequel cards are still laid out on the table or floor.

First, review the self-inventory cards you prepared as part of your work in chapter three. Make sure the story you have now planned is compatible with your perceived strengths and weaknesses, your most dearly held values, your favorite kind of person, and so on. I'll hope that they are! If you discover that you may be planning to write a story vastly different from your real favorite type, or deviating from your inventory in some other basic way, you need to review your thinking; either the story you've planned is not the best for you, or your perceptions of "story" have changed as you studied intermediate chapters.

Think about it, and if you find deviation, make sure you're aware of it, have good reason for the perceived deviation, and want to continue on the present course. The alternative—which writers seldom take at this juncture because of haste or impatience—would be to go take a new self-inventory, or revise your story plans as reflected in the scene-sequel cards. Don't overlook the possibility that the work and learning you've done so far might have changed your writing goals and procedures so much by this point that you do need to revise some earlier planning.

Having completed this creative self-check, you are ready to move on.

The next step is to look over the tag and trait cards prepared in chapter four, and decide which of these you plan to use for the characters you have set up for the currently planned story. You may already have these cards arranged under the scenes in which the characters first appear, as we talked about the possibility of doing this as part of our self-checking work in chapter nine.

If you already have the cards in place, take a few minutes at least to reconsider each character and his role in the story, and make sure you don't have a better character or partial character languishing in the file box when a useful substitution might be made at this stage.

If you hadn't yet put character cards in the plan, do so now. Place the selected character beneath the card outlining the first scene in which that character is to appear—sort of the way you would arrange cards in a game of solitaire.

You now have the skeleton plan for your cast arranged in the block-diagram order of the scenes and sequels.

Next, go through your cards again, looking for those you prepared on your characters as part of the work assigned in chapter six. Again, pull useful cards out of the shoebox inventory and clip each useful one to the card you just laid down to indicate where a given character enters the story. You are now fleshing out the people you plan to use in this particular story.

Finally, in terms of your story people, examine the cards you prepared for chapter ten on deepening your characters. If you find a card (or cards) that amplifies some aspect of the story characters already arrayed in your card layout, pull such cards and attach *them*, too, to the character cards already spread out.

In chapter seven you made decisions about the setting for this story. Review the cards on setting that you filled out at that time, and pull any cards with descriptions or factual data you plan to use in this story.

Make an attempt to arrange any such setting cards under the card for the scene or sequel where you believe you will introduce the material. For any data you aren't sure of in terms of placement, just arrange those off to one side under a new header card titled *Setting*.

Refer to all the character work you did in chapter eight. If you find anything amiss in your character plans as they now are reflected by the cards on the table, make the necessary changes.

Although it will not provide any subsidiary new cards to your fleshed-out layout, let me suggest that you briefly review chapter five concerning kinds of story, and clarify in your mind what type this story most resembles. A card should be filled out with the word *Conflict* or *Decision* or *Discovery* on it, to keep you reminded generally of the kind of story you are working on. This card can be put on the table above all the others, just as a reminder.

There may be other cards lurking in your shoebox that you want to pull out and arrange somewhere on your table at this point. In going through your earlier work in search of specifics, you have undoubtedly refreshed your memory in some areas not mentioned in this present chapter. So if you find any cards you want to add, feel free to do so.

Having done all this, you have your complete planning guide laid out on the table or floor. Alternatively, some people paste cards on the wall of their workroom, in the same general pattern. Some take the additional step of transferring all the information on all the cards into a detailed story block diagram at this point. Neither moving the cards nor making a block diagram on separate paper is necessary; you can do it, however, if it would make you feel more secure. (I had a student once who got this far, then accidentally let his dog into the office. The dog ate quite a number of cards . . . so possibly there could be more than *emotional* security involved here if you decide to duplicate your card work on separate sheets of paper.)

## CHECKING THE ENDING

As you surely have noticed by this time, the one aspect of your story that we haven't addressed in any detail during this laying out of cards is how the story is to end. There was a method in that madness; your first job was to concentrate on knowing what the story question is, and finding an ending sure to answer the question as asked. However, before you've taken the last step in your fine tuning, perhaps you will want to consider filling out one or more cards to place at the very end of your string of scene-sequel cards, that new category being labeled *Climax/Ending*.

This card (or cards) will briefly outline what is to take place in the final scene or sequel.

You should prepare a new major category card to be placed directly beneath the "Climax/Ending" card. Atop this one you should write the answer to the story question—and make sure it *answers* the story question. Then, on one or more additional cards, you should outline, step by step, what happens in this final scene or sequel—and make sure that the event or thoughts you have planned clearly provide the answer you wrote down.

The ending is all-important. It will leave your reader satisfied or frustrated. It will provide the final "taste" of the story left with your reader. It will sum up, condense, symbolize, or otherwise become the total meaning of the story. It must be right.

There are a few general principles you should consider in laying out this climax/ending scene or sequel.

### If the Ending Is a Scene

1. You should attempt to make it the most highly dramatic in the story. That may mean the most explosive physical action, the most intense emotional conflict, the most painful confrontation, or something similar.

2. You should have your protagonist and antagonist onstage for this confrontation, with all the chips finally on the table.

3. Both participants should clearly realize that this is the ultimate scene where everything is to be gained or lost.

4. Time pressure should drive both participants, if you can devise

such an element. (Ask yourself, "What have I plotted here that makes it impossible for either of them to back away and plan to fight again another day?")

5. Whatever final words you may need after the scene to give it meaning or clarity should be very, very brief. You must guard against last-line pontificating or anticlimax.

## If the Ending Is a Sequel

1. Ninety-nine times out of a hundred, you must be in the viewpoint of your protagonist. In the rare case where you show the defeated antagonist, or require another actor to state some meaning, their preoccupation must be with the meaning *for the protagonist* more than themselves.

2. You should be especially aware that "purple prose" — overinflated or flowery writing — is more likely to occur in the sequel ending than anywhere else in the story. Strive for a simple, direct, brief conclusion.

3. You cannot foist onto the reader some meaning that does not clearly grow out of the action that preceded it in the story. Make sure to avoid "lecturing about meaning" at the very end.

4. You should be alert for possible loose threads that a sequel might briefly tie up; look for secondary problems for the main character that the reader might still worry about, or problems existing for some supporting character that should be addressed.

5. Long explanations are to be avoided at all costs.

## SUMMARY

You are now in position to review all previous planning, and integrate that work into your card-diagram for the story you are about to write. This should be done by arranging additional cards under the scene-sequel cards arrayed earlier.

Timing, setting and other aspects of the story should be reviewed in terms of your likes and dislikes to make sure everything is in order.

Special attention can be paid to the ending at this time. A detailed outline of that ending may be in order.

You should always bear in mind that most earlier decisions are still fairly easy to correct or change at this time. Inasmuch as you are about to launch into the writing of a first draft, this final look at plotting the "big picture" may be helpful to you in spotting and correcting any flaws. You may wish to translate all your card work into a block diagram of some kind, but it isn't necessary . . . unless you have a card-eating pet!

## Chapter Thirteen

# Writing Your First Draft

---

**PROGRESS CHECK:**

✔ *Are all your scene-sequel cards laid out in proper storytelling order?*

✔ *Are all subsidiary cards arrayed beneath them?*

✔ *Have you given extra thought to the ending?*

✔ *Are you—by this time—aching to write the story?*

✔ *Then you are ready.*

---

B y this time, you have come to know the characters who will people your story, and you've developed a strong, working map or outline of your plot—the emotional and physical obstacle course your characters must face. You've put in many hours of careful, sometimes tedious planning.

Now it's time for the payoff. This chapter signals the point where all your planning, thinking, researching and organizing begin to take more satisfying shape.

It's time for you to write your first full draft of the story.

Perhaps you feel a bit uneasy about taking this major step. But you shouldn't be. If you have done all the preliminary work outlined in previous chapters, you are ready. Any hesitancy or uncertainty you may feel at this late date is just the normal slight worry that any writer faces any time she begins a first draft.

You are as ready as you're going to get. It's time for action.

In fact, you have a distinct advantage over students in the novel classes I taught for many years at the University of Oklahoma. There, on the first day of class, I walked in and gave them the date (in about fourteen weeks) when I expected at least 50,000 words of first draft of a novel. I pointed out that they had better start writing *now*.

Some of them practically went into shock at this point. A lot of them had never undertaken any major writing project, and certainly not a novel. They were intimidated. They were also puzzled: "How," they would ask, "can I start writing a novel when I haven't had any instruction yet?"

My response to them was essentially what I want to say to reassure you now.

You probably started out in this map knowing more about short-story writing than you realized. We — writers like you and me — are readers. We know a lot about short fiction from reading it, whether we know that we know.

Furthermore, you're going to have to write a first draft sooner or later, and if you feel uneasy now, you'll likely feel no better about the chore a month from now. All writers are a little scared of that blank page. The only difference between the professional and the amateur is that the professional ignores the uncertainty and starts writing, confident that the planning has already assured the best story she's capable of producing at this time.

Also, remember that you can always go back and revise your first draft. *Any* words you put on paper now will be better than none at all.

And despite all the planning we've done, some problems will still arise in every story: We won't like a character we thought we would like, or we'll become dissatisfied with our style, or we'll find we need more setting information, or *something*. Some of these problems can't be anticipated; we have to launch into a first draft to discover them.

So you're far more ready than you realize, you can always plan to fix any mistakes that may creep in at this point, and some problems can only be discovered through the writing process itself. *There is no reason to delay.*

It may further reassure you to think back to some of the concepts you have already absorbed here in the Map. You have a much clearer idea of the kinds of stories you want to write. You have a knowledge of how such stories are researched and structured. You've been observing real people, listening to real conversations, and enriching your "toolbox" of character cards. You understand that fictional characters must be vivid and bigger than life. You understand how conflict tests and creates character, and adversity creates sympathy. And you now see that the essence of good fiction is *movement* — often in the physical sense, but certainly in the emotional sense: A story starts one place and ends up somewhere else.

You know, too, that a story begins with a story question and ends when that question is answered.

And you have planned with all these things in mind. You have stacks of file cards on dialogue, character appearance, setting, structure, and everything else that goes into a good story.

Clearly it's time to put self-doubt aside and start making pages.

## STORY STARTERS

As you get under way, let your unconscious mind dwell on the following two factors: the way a good story begins, and the way a good story concludes. For if you have started at the right place, and know where you want to go, you're 90 percent sure of doing things right.

Let's look at story starters from a slightly different perspective than we assumed before, but one that you will now understand clearly.

We talked earlier about story question and answer. In chapter ten, we also discussed the character's *self-concept*, and how vital that is in understanding the character. Perhaps at that time you sensed how closely linked story question and self-concept can be.

If the story character, like any real-life person, seeks to preserve and enhance his concept of himself, the most threatening and motivating development that can befall the character is anything that threatens the self-concept. And what can most threaten the self-concept?

Change.

For example, your character Marie has spent her adult life seeing herself as a wife and mother. But now her last child leaves home, she no longer has motherly duties, and her husband has grown so engrossed in his office work that he seldom treats her as a wife. Marie feels threatened, if not devastated. Why? Because her circumstances no longer support her concept of herself. She still *thinks* and *feels* like a wife and mother; but she sees no evidence in her daily life that she *is* a wife and mother today.

If you were to write a story about Marie, it would make sense to start the story — pose the story question — at the moment she finally realizes, "Wait a minute! Things have changed and my self-concept doesn't feel comfortable any more."

Marie, in other words, would be threatened by change. If she is worth writing about, she won't just sit around and be uncomfortable or miserable; she will figure out something she has to do, or think about, or discover, that will reestablish some sort of equilibrium between herself, her world and her self-concept.

Of course she won't think of it in these terms. But she will struggle, even if she doesn't know why. And when she feels threatened, and starts to struggle, her saga has begun.

Or to put it another way: Change is where your story starts.

The moral, then, is simple. If uneasiness, worry or outright fear seem to stop you from actually starting your rough draft, go back and study your laid-out cards once more. Refresh your perception of what your viewpoint character is like, what his self-concept is. (If you have not clearly defined his self-concept on a card, by all means do so immediately.)

Having done this, examine the card outlining the proposed opening of your story. Ask yourself the following questions:

1. Does this opening clearly demonstrate a change of some kind that has very recently—or is currently—altering circumstances in the viewpoint character's life in such a way that his self-concept is threatened?

2. Have I set up this self-concept threat to be as intense, vivid and distressing as possible for the viewpoint character?

3. Is my opening threat situation of a type that allows the viewpoint character to make *some* sort of effort to rectify the situation, or prevent further frightening change, or seek the advice of someone else, or take some action almost at once, or *do something* in response to what has just befallen him?

Your answer to each of these questions should be an unequivocal "yes." Your opening change might be the loss of a job, a divorce, a wedding, an unexpected letter, a telephone call, the falling of a leaf, an earthquake, or an unanticipated cross word from a loved one. It might, in other words, be anything at all as long as it passed the three-question crisis test listed above.

Thinking about story openings in this way can sometimes jumpstart your imagination. To state the problem in a different way, you have been having trouble actually starting to commit first-draft words to paper, you might be suffering opening-night jitters—which you must ignore and press on—or you might not yet have identified precisely the right opening sentences. It's the second reason for getting hung up at the outset that readdressing character, self-concept and opening situation may correct.

A writer I once knew told me that she started planning every story she had ever written with a person getting off a train or bus in the middle of the night, in a strange town, and starting up the dark and lonely street carrying a suitcase.

How many stories had she actually published with this opening?

Not one. Visualizing that moment of *change* simply got her thinking clearly about what the character lacked and needed. Beginning her thought before the word processor with this scene of change in her mind immediately freed her imagination to see her character more clearly, and get him into motion that would soon actually start her story.

Find the moment of change and start writing from that point. Be sure to make the story question clear as early as possible. Everything else will follow.

A final word for now about starting the draft. It's all too easy to postpone work until tomorrow, or the day after that. Weeks can pass . . . months . . . years. Successful writers work today, tomorrow and the day after that. Failures talk about writing "someday," but never seem to find the time.

So start! *Any* words put on paper at this point are an advancement.

## THE MIDDLE OF YOUR STORY

A good work attitude, as alluded to in the two paragraphs above, can go amazingly far toward solving problems for the writer as she plows ahead into the murky uncertainty of her first draft. (Believe me, no matter how much planning we have done to this point, there will still be moments when you are almost overcome with doubt; they're normal, and must be worked through.) The people who seem to have the most trouble with confusion and self-doubts during the creation of a story draft seem to be those whose work habits leave something to be desired.

Regular exposure to your story on a daily basis, even if for a relatively short time each day, will go far toward easing your problems. When you face the story each day, even if for only an hour or so, you keep it toward the front of your conscious mind. Even more important, you keep it foremost in your creative mind, and in your unconscious. If you will maintain a regular work schedule, your unconscious mind—constantly prodded to muse about the story—will work out some of your problems without your even thinking about them on a conscious level.

The person who tries to hit a creative lick one weekend, perhaps, then two weeks later, gives up this advantage of conscious and unconscious preoccupation. She has to start "cold" every time she sits down at the machine. In the worst cases, she forgets where she was in the story, or what feelings she was trying to portray when she last wrote. She may even forget where she was exactly in the plot! Such intermittent work habits form a recipe for creative disaster.

The lesson should be clear. Good work habits, as you move through your draft, are vital. Stay with the project daily. It is far better to write one page of a rough draft daily, six days a week, than it is to take off five or six days, then try to catch up by writing ten pages on Sunday.

Although you have a great many tasks ahead of you as you write a draft, you may find it helpful to do what some of my students have done. They tack a calendar to the wall near the desk, and record their word or page output in every daily block. This "visual conscience" keeps them from making excuses for themselves, letting days of creative inactivity go by.

Be realistic in planning how much you will do each day. It's better to establish a schedule that's a bit too easy than to set up an extremely ambitious one you're doomed to rarely meet.

And by all means set some sort of regular *production quota*, rather than a daily allocation of time. If you tell yourself you'll work from two to four o'clock every afternoon, for example, chances are that you'll find yourself spending a lot of that two hours staring at the wall, or at your cards, or at the lint in your navel. Then, after two hours and virtually no work, you'll get up and go on to something else, wondering why you seem to be hung up.

If you have a production quota, on the other hand, you will know that you plan to force yourself to stay at the desk every day until you have produced, say, three pages. Or six. The first two or three days, you might find that you have to spend an ungodly amount of time at the word processor to meet your self-imposed quota. But a funny thing will happen very quickly. Once convinced that you mean it, that you intend to stick to the chair until the pages have been produced, your imagination will start working faster and more smoothly to get body and soul *both* out of that hard chair as soon as possible.

I have known writers who began with a four-hour daily writing schedule, and produced two or three pages a week. Once they changed their quota to a certain number of pages, they found that their daily production soon shot sky high—and took far less time.

Also, please note an important caveat here. When I speak of a daily production quota of pages—be it two or ten—I am speaking of *newly created* pages. Don't fool yourself into thinking you're accomplishing much by going back over the same four or five pages every day, allegedly fine-tuning the language. What you're really doing is screwing up your production schedule. Your job at this point is to produce new, fresh pages—and to get a complete first draft into the box. Fixing comes later.

Keep looking at your planning cards. Frequently review the cards outlining the story question and its answer. This will keep you on track.

Refer often to the character cards, too, as you move along. Keep your characters consistent with the card profiles.

Stay with your sequence of scene-sequel or plot cards, or your block diagram, if you have by now translated all the cards into such a large diagram. Beware of a sudden burst of inspiration at this point! If you *must* think about some wild new idea for the story that occurs during the first draft, stop work on the story long enough to outline the inspiration on cards or in a separate computer file, then go back and forge ahead with your story as you already planned it.

Why should this be your intention? Because "great ideas" that come during the writing of a draft are often based on nothing but the playfulness of the imagination; they can often send your carefully planned story onto some wild plot vector from which you can never recover; such ideas have *nothing* to do with all the planning you've already done, and may actually represent a hidden revolt by a tiring imagination, which always prefers aimless play or daydreaming to disciplined work.

Once you have finished the draft, you can always go back and reexamine that "great idea" you had. If it still seems wonderful, perhaps you will want to work it into your planning cards and revise your story accordingly. Even if you do that, you will be doing it at the right time, with a certain degree of forethought—and not just because this strange idea leaped into your head while you were wearily spell-checking Thursday's output.

If you start getting hung up on how your words look on the page, or how they seem to sound in your head, welcome to the writer's club. I think everyone has these moments of self-doubt. But this is no time to stop writing and get all messed up on word choice or questions such as, "Do I use two sentences or three to get him from his home to the bus stop?" Press on! Anything can be fixed later.

(Have I said that before???)

If you get to a scene or sequel that really seems impossible to write in full at this point in first draft, simply push yourself ahead by typing a condensed version of the segment, or outline words, or the part you do see clearly. Then keep going. Your momentum is everything at this point.

As mentioned before, however, you should avoid the habit of always skipping the hard parts, and only writing the few scenes you have earlier imagined most vividly. Writers who skip through a draft, writing only the fun or easy parts, often find that going back and filling in *all* the hard parts is really dreadful drudgery, and not any fun because all the fun stuff has already been produced. So skipping a scene or sequel to maintain progress in your work is a relatively rare gambit, and writing the "best scenes" first may sometimes fuel your enthusiasm, but can easily become a trap.

Remember, too, to produce your pages in sequential order, as planned. Don't jump from planned scene 2 to planned scene 4 because scene 4 will be more fun to write. You've got to write it all eventually anyhow, and jumping around is as bad as skipping all the hard parts. Many writers keep themselves motivated to grind through some days' or weeks' weary labor because they can see that—once they get through this part—they will have that really vivid, fun scene to write.

To put this another way, if you pick out the fun parts to write first, or skip around to find them, you are, in the process, removing your internal motivation to write the hard parts.

## THOUGHTS TO HELP YOU PRESS ON

Here are some other observations about the first-draft process which might help you.

I've said it before, but it should be remembered always: Good stories aren't written; they're rewritten. No matter how bad you may feel about the pages you produce today, they're better than no pages at all. You can always fix them later. Your job at the moment is to produce *something* concrete, which you can revise later.

False starts, messy transitions, recalcitrant characters, and all manner of other disasters befall every writer during first draft. Pros don't let this discourage or frighten them.

Most excuses for not writing are not good enough.

Usually when a writer gets stuck in first draft, it's because (a) she has strayed somehow from the story question or (b) he has stopped having anything happen at all. If stuck, you should look hard at the story question card and the story-ending card, and ask yourself how this place where you are right now *directly contributes* to the progress from one card to the other. If you can't find a direct causal link, you've gotten off track and have to go back and plan a different scene or sequel that will reestablish progress. If you have stopped the action and reaction entirely—and fallen into a description of a static state or unchanging emotion or unmoving bit of setting, *stop doing that instantly* and get on with the story.

Fatigue is cumulative. You can't give in to it entirely because some of it is inevitable during the trial of writing a story draft. However, you can take steps to minimize it both physically and mentally.

A walk around the block, a bicycle ride, a game of golf, or almost any physical *fun* activity will restore you physically. Even when you feel the most tired, it's probably the kind of fatigue that comes from sitting at the machine and hitting the keys. More beneficial physical exercise—movement that stirs the blood a little—can have amazing curative results even when one starts it with a draggy, feeling of reluctance. Many writers I know belong to a health club of some kind because membership provides a regular place and time for workouts.

Mental tiredness may also be treated through physical exercise. You might also look for other activities to engage the mind in a different way, however—a bridge game, perhaps, or a good movie, or a lively conversation with an old friend.

Such activities are not self-indulgence.

## STORY FINISHERS

Given all that has just been said about getting stuck, hung up, or overtired during the middle of a story, it seems paradoxical that something must also be said about the story that never seems ready to end. I've known writers who set out to write a 3,000-word short story and came back weeks later practically in tears because they were now at the 10,000-word mark and "I can't get everything wound up—I can't find the ending for all this!"

It would be simple enough to suggest sticking the answer to the story question onto the next scene, but it's seldom as easy as that.

Sometimes writers are *afraid* to end the story draft . . . because that would mean they have to revise it, and face the eventual possibility of rejection.

Sometimes writers like the characters so much that they don't want to let the story end—to let the creative fun stop.

And sometimes writers can't finish a story because in the writing of the draft they have inadvertently discovered a flaw in their original planning.

There used to be a yellowed old copy of a Peanuts cartoon strip on my office door at the University of Oklahoma. The cartoon panels showed Snoopy atop his doghouse, at his typewriter:

"And so his life ended as it had begun," Snoopy had written, "a failure.

He had wanted love. He found only hate.

He had wanted fame. He found obscurity.

He had wanted wealth. He was poor."

At which point Snoopy looks up and thinks, "I'm having a hard time ending this."

Poor Snoopy. He was having trouble ending the story because his original story concept was faulty. The hero's goal was too vague, so there could be no clear story question. Since there could be no clear story question, there could be no clear, satisfying answer. Since the hero apparently had never had a plan, he had never had a chance. Since he had never had a chance, his story couldn't be brought to a satisfactory conclusion.

If you find yourself having difficulty with ending the first draft, my first advice is not to worry too much about it. You can simply stop where you seem stuck, if you must, and study the situation later, for revision.

Whether you stop then or decide to fight the problem immediately, however, you might make sure first that you're not stuck because you're scared or too enamored of the characters or something like that—some internal writer's problem. If you discover such an internal psychological problem, simply recognizing it usually frees you to move beyond it.

If you don't discover any such problem with yourself or your attitudes, however, think deeply about poor Snoopy, atop his dog-house, wanting to end a story that never had a question, written about a character who never really had a chance.

Long odds and severe conflict are great in a story. But it's possible to make the story problem unsolvable . . . the quest impossible. If you've done that, it's time to go back and study all your cards. You had a faulty concept. The trouble with the ending made this clear to you.

Don't feel bad if you make such a discovery of faulty concept. This kind of discovery by the writer is very common. For example, in one of my recent novels, *Double Fault* (Tor Books), the premise had to do with a man who had committed an understandable but regrettable act in Vietnam long ago. My assumption about the ending was that he would be fully exonerated at last. However, as I wrote the book and neared the ending, I came to feel more and more ambivalence about his act and whether he *should* be exonerated. This gave me all sorts of trouble with the ending, of course, because I couldn't find a way to answer the story question clearly enough, and I saw that the character's quest might have been doomed from the outset. Finally I solved the problem by going back to the first premise of the book and changing the circumstances of my character's act and its aftermath. The change was small—adding a heavy burden of personal guilt to him—but it provided a way to write a story ending that answered the question about that guilt and how he would spend the rest of his life dealing with it.

Finally, one additional word about the ending. Do not—repeat, do *not*—fall victim to the temptation to tell the reader what the ending means, or what "moral" he might draw from it. A good story must stand on its own. Many almost-good stories have been ruined at the very end by moral preachments or sermons by well-meaning authors who suddenly forgot that their job is to portray realistic people in dramatic situations—and not to peddle philosophy.

In a good story, the meaning will come through the action. In a bad story in which this doesn't happen as an inevitable dynamic of fiction, no amount of preaching can help a whit.

## SUMMARY

Although a writer may feel some trepidation about starting to write a first draft of a story, such uncertainty is normal and must be worked through. Reexamination of planning cards and block diagrams should give you heart for the task ahead. You *are* ready.

A problem in opening the story should be solved by checking the character's self-concept and goal one more time, and selecting a moment of crucial change as the opening scene of the story.

Good work habits—a regular daily page or word quota—will keep you on track once you have gotten underway. Worries along the way should be put aside insofar as possible. It may help to remember that your job at this point is to produce pages. You can fix problems later.

The ending of a story must answer the story question. This is accomplished *not* through author commentary or preaching, but through thought, feeling or action by the viewpoint character. If the story works at all, the meaning will out.

*Chapter Fourteen*

# Avoiding Pitfalls During a First Draft

---

PROGRESS CHECK:

✔ *Are you ignoring fears and pressing on with the draft on a regular quota basis?*

✔ *Are you sticking to your plans as shown on your cards?*

---

The last chapter dealt with a great many possible pitfalls for the writer embarked on the stormy seas of a first story draft. There are only a few others that perhaps should be mentioned at this point as you continue producing your pages.

Let's take a brief look at some of these other pitfalls that could impede your progress through a rough draft.

## TALKING TOO MUCH ABOUT THE STORY

Any number of writers in the past have warned against talking too much about a story in progress. The usual reason given for this warning has been the idea that you might "talk it right out of your system" — expend so much energy and enthusiasm talking about the story that you don't have enough creative energy left to write it. This can indeed happen, and the advice remains good: While writing your draft, don't talk about it with anyone unless it happens to be a professional writer who is tutoring you.

Another problem with talking about your story is that you might find yourself changing details—adding or subtracting—to please your listener of the moment. When telling your closest friend about a romance story, for example, you might emphasize the most explicit parts of the romance. But in telling your maiden aunt about it, you might elide those parts almost entirely, and talk instead about the story atmosphere or setting. Talk of this nature — changing to fit individual audience preference — can muddle your vision of the story.

Closely related to this kind of self-sabotage is telling your story to an admired friend or colleague, and watching carefully for his reactions. Maybe he frowns when you tell him of some plot development, so you go back to the word processor with your confidence shaken in that part of the story. You may even decide to change it. Or perhaps he smiles and applauds at some aspect you mention when you thought that was a minor point; again, his reaction may motivate you to make a change that's not at all what you had planned, or what may be best for the story.

One more reason that talking about a story in progress is bad: When you're talking about it, you're not working on it. Enough said.

## ASKING FOR ADVICE

Closely related to talking about the story is asking someone — or some group of someones — for advice about it. Such advice, if given, is seldom honest; most friends and acquaintances will tell you the story is wonderful even if inwardly they are bored out of their minds. They want to be nice . . . and don't want to hurt your feelings.

Worse, they may actually *give* you advice. And what in the world ever made you think they know more about your story than you do? They are not reading it like an impartial editor or magazine reader; their judgment is colored at best, and unless they are much published, frankly they don't know what they're talking about.

Although I admire many of the things they accomplish, writers clubs sometimes do real damage to writers in this regard. Some, as you know, function by having members bring material to meetings for criticism. I have seen writers read part of a draft and eagerly await comments. Such activity is almost always doomed to be counterproductive.

In the first place, writers go to these meetings and *read their work aloud*. This is a performance. It in no way resembles the experience a reader might have, reading the words on paper. Some writers are good readers, and could make a grocery list sound entrancing. Others could read from *Paradise Lost* and make it sound like drivel. Reading a work is not like giving it to a neutral person to read — it's even worse.

Further, I have seen writers go to such meetings and read from work in progress — and then be hit by a tornado of conflicting comment. Some people belong to writers clubs, it seems, to prove to themselves how superior they are. Whenever anyone reads, these egomaniacs leap up to point out everything wrong with the work. Sometimes their points are well taken and sometimes they aren't, but in no case does such nasty, destructive criticism help.

Other club critics are the opposite. They always say every work is wonderful. They find meanings that aren't there, praise prose they haven't seen, and predict great successes when even a fine story may ultimately enjoy only a modest publication and payment.

Whatever the case, the poor story-reader leaves confused and battered.

Writers clubs have many good functions. Some of their education programs are first-rate, and even a poor functioning club may serve a useful purpose in providing a place where lonely and insecure writers can go and find some solace in friendly talk and camaraderie.

Taking work in progress for reading aloud, however, can be deadly.

Save asking for advice, if you do at all, until much later, when you consider the story finished. Then, if you know a seasoned professional writer who does some coaching, or perhaps a teacher with real experience in the world of publishing, perhaps you can consider taking the work to him or her. You may in such a case get some good information about your work.

Even then, however, a bit of a warning. I have had experiences with New York publishers that show even a pro's opinion probably isn't the only valid one. I have had one editor tell me a story was "impossible" or unpublishable, and the next editor offer me a pleasing amount of money for it. One person's meat is another's poison. Take *all* advice with skepticism.

(The only ironclad exception to this prohibition might be when an editor sends you a contract or check, then says she wants some minor changes. My personal evaluation of such situations is that an editor with checkbook in hand usually should be listened to.)

## WORRYING ABOUT THE FATE OF THE MANUSCRIPT

It's inevitable to worry about where you're going to send the finished story, and especially whether anyone is going to buy it. Excessive worry along these lines during the writing process, however, can be paralyzing. Remember that you have done some market study and some self-analysis. If you sense that you may be worrying too much along these lines, take time out and review your market cards and self-inventory cards. They will assure you that you're on the right track, having done so much planning. Then you can continue, keeping the worries about ultimate outcome on the back burner as much as possible.

## DECIDING SOME NEW IDEA IS FAR BETTER

This is an amazingly common problem, especially during first draft. You get a little tired, you hit a snag or two, you've stared at your own copy so intently that it looks and sounds awkward to you—and out of the blue a new story idea begins to build. You find yourself thinking about it in bed at night. "Wow," you think. "This idea is ten times better than the story I'm working on!"

So do you abandon work on the story in progress and plunge headlong into the new and more wonderful idea?

My God, no. No, no, no, no.

New and different ideas will come during your writing of the present story, especially during first draft work when uncertainty makes you vulnerable to doubt and receptive to *any* thought that gives you an excuse to opt out of further painful work. When such ideas come, recognize them for tricks of the lazy imagination, which would rather play with a new idea than doggedly working through the present project in a disciplined fashion. Stick with your present work!

If the new idea continues to bother you, by all means take out two or three fresh cards—maximum—and jot down the idea or the briefest possible plot synopsis. Start a new category in your file box titled *Ideas*. Put the card or cards in there. Then get back to work on what you're supposed to be doing.

This way you will not lose the new idea. You will not sabotage or abandon the currect project. And, surprisingly, your unconscious will work better on the new idea, even as you proceed on the present one, because you have put it safely on cards and filed it. Nothing is lost, everything is gained.

## DOING TOO MUCH LEISURE READING

This may sound strange. But there are two major dangers in reading a lot of fiction while producing your own fiction draft.

One danger is discouragement, as you may read something wonderful, and despair of ever being able to do such fine work.

The second danger lies in unrealized imitation.

Many writers have told me about this latter danger, and I have experienced it myself. One of my favorite authors is Jack Higgins. I never read a Jack Higgins novel while writing a draft of something of my own. If I do, the closeness to Higgins makes my style start sounding too much like his . . . my characters as chill and frightening as some of his, even when it is not my intent.

The lesson here: While most writers tend to be voracious readers, they should avoid too much fiction reading during the crucial time of writing their own first draft. Once they have a draft in the copy box and the die is more or less cast for the story in its major proportions, they can perhaps risk reading more of others' work while going on with their own project.

## FALLING PREY TO SELF-DOUBT

Show me a writer who has not experienced discouragement and profound self-doubt, and I'll show you a writer who never tried to produce fiction.

"Maybe I don't have the talent," you may think during the writing of page six. Or, "Maybe I wasn't cut out for this." Or, perhaps worst of all, "This stuff I'm writing here sounds really dumb."

In more than twenty years of dealing with writing students, I think I have heard the fear about "sounding dumb" about ten zillion times. Such doubts come from fatigue and a driving ambition, which sometimes combine to make the present words on paper appear far less than the writer wishes they could be.

Self-doubt—as has been said here on numerous occasions—is normal for a writer. During first draft work, difficulties tend to multiply, making the writer even more vulnerable to self-doubt than during the planning or revision stage. Sometimes writers get so enmeshed in self-doubt that they stop work. You must not let this happen.

## MAINTAINING A POSITIVE ATTITUDE

These and many other fears and hang-ups of all kinds can be lessened to a remarkable degree by following a very simple program, which uses what I call dream cards.

Take out a fresh card. On the card, write something very much like the following:

I am working on my best story.
This story is going to be great.
This story will sell.
I am going to succeed.

Take out a second card. On that card, in your own words, describe in about twenty-five words how some editor is going to rhapsodize about this story when you submit it to her.

Take out a third card. Lean back in a comfortable chair for a few minutes and imagine, as vividly as possible, how you are going to feel when you have achieved the things you want to achieve as a writer. *See* this future life you will have. Believe in it.

If you believe in any kind of deity, thank him or her in advance for making it possible that this dream *will* come true.

After this imagining, take the third card and briefly write down how great you feel to know what lies ahead for you.

This is an exercise that will banish fear and self-doubt. If you will pardon another autobiographical note, it is one that kept me going for ten years of nonpublication before the great thrill of selling my first book. Your dream can come true if you believe in and work toward it. It not only can, but will.

Maintaining faith, working on, is the real definition of talent.

When you have finished your draft — which is sure to be far better than you ever imagined it could be — you can turn to chapter fifteen.

## SUMMARY

There are many ways a writer can falter during the difficult task of writing a first draft, and there are many mistakes she can make that only make matters worse. Some of these have to do with losing faith and seeking the advice of others who know far less than she does.

Maintaining faith is not always easy, but it can — and must — become a habit for you as a writer. Even in this area the use of filing cards may provide a vehicle for remembering how the future can be.

## Chapter Fifteen

# Revising Your Copy, Part I

---

PROGRESS CHECK:

✔ *Is the first draft finished and "in the box" — printed out in its entirety?*

---

Congratulations!

You have completed a first draft.

That means you've already done more than 99 percent of the people who say they want to be a writer. You're a writer now, perhaps more so than you ever were before, even if you had written a great many stories, because this time you have have produced a first draft in the most professional manner possible.

But now, of course, there's a catch. You've got to do some revision. And you're probably a little tired at this point. Try to remember that the scariest part is already behind you. You now have pages on which to work. You have worked through the worst time of confusion and self-doubt. Now you're going to hone and polish and recast, perhaps — a little — to finish a story that's probably better than the one you imagined weeks ago, in the first flush of your enthusiasm for the new idea.

None of this is to suggest that fiction revision is easy. It isn't. For one thing, all of us hate to change our own precious copy. But by developing a systematic plan for revision, and working to maintain our critical but positive attitude, revision can be far less harrowing than it otherwise might be — and far more beneficial.

So let's take a look at the revision process.

It probably is an oversimplification to say that revision is a two-part process. Sometimes, during revision we may begin to feel that it's a thousand-part process! But generally speaking revision falls into two broad categories, which are quite different and should be approached in different ways and at different times.

The first category of revision involves work we know needs doing even as we finish the first draft. This kind of work is the stuff we have realized that we'll have to do, even as we make our draft pages. As mentioned in the last chapter, we don't often stop to go back and fix something during the white heat of original creation; either we remember it, make a marginal note about it in our printout and keep on going, or perhaps jot a note or two on a revision card. At any rate, even in stories that go very well during the initial process of creation, we're likely to have a number of such fixes clearly in mind as we write. You may decide partway through the draft to change a character's appearance, for example, or you discover a better speech tag. Or maybe you notice that you're going to have to slip in another paragraph or two of information about the setting to prepare the reader for some later event. You may have decided as you wrote that two character names sounded too similar, and that one will have to be changed on revision.

Such repairs can be done as soon after completion of the first draft as you feel ready to tackle them. You can — and should — go back through the manuscript and make these promptly.

Remember, however, that your goal at this point is not a finished or clean manuscript. If you notice other problems as you do your "rough carpentry work," you may wish to mark them with one of your colored pencils, perhaps marking plot problems in red, characters who need work in green, and so on. It's also perfectly OK to jot down minor factual corrections at this time, too, just sticking them in with Scotch tape. If you work on a computer or word processor, I don't recommend even reprinting the draft just yet. Simply insert needed obvious repairs, if you wish to go a bit past the penciling stage now, and keep on plugging.

This obvious, factual kind of correction may take a few hours or somewhat longer. As with writing the draft, however, you should continue to maintain a regular work schedule. However, it will not be possible to set yourself the same kind of rigid work quota that you used during the writing. You might be able to go through and pencil in a name change in minutes, for example. On the other hand, you might have to go back to the library or check into the

Internet to ascertain some information you just realized you need, and that could take hours or even days.

## LETTING THINGS COOL DOWN

Once you have finished such obvious revisions, you may have a manuscript that looks like somebody's crazy idea of a paper accordion—extra sheets or half-sheets folded in, insertions sticking out at odd angles, a page here or there cut with scissors to eliminate some inconsistency, so it isn't even full-length anymore. If you're on the computer or word processor, of course, you won't have such a physical mess, but you'll certainly have a different text file. Retype or reprint the manuscript at this point if you want to, but you may want to wait.

Your next job during Part I of revision is to let the manuscript—and the author—cool down a bit. You need to establish a little space between yourself and this intense work you just completed.

What this means is that you need to get away from the manuscript for at least a week.

Why? Every writer knows that it's almost impossible to see your work as a "cold" reader would see it. Sometimes we read meanings into our own copy that aren't sufficiently suggested. Sometimes we fall in love with our own prose when we shouldn't. Sometimes, because of fatigue and a gap between original story conception and almost-finished product, we are disappointed and feel negative and *hate* how our words look on paper. And of course there is always some element of suspense and curiosity in every story, and there is no way we can read our own story with the same kind of curiosity and tension that an unknowing reader might experience.

A break from your manuscript for a week or two will not work magic. You still won't experience the story in the way a cold reader will see it. In my own career, I have had the dismaying realization that I have to put about *twenty years* between the creation and the reading if I am really to begin to see the story as others can see it.

Well, obviously we don't have twenty years to let the story cool off. But we can benefit greatly from even a week's "vacation" from it if we employ the cooling-off time in a constructive way.

So your first job at this point is to put your pages in a desk drawer and vow not to look at them again for a week or so. Second, you should turn your block diagrams face-down on the worktable, or find an old sheet and drape it over your card layout so you won't see any of *that* for a few days, either.

Now you have the project out of sight, but probably still not out of mind. You may catch yourself brooding about the story and even thinking of some new revision ideas. If so, there's nothing wrong with taking out a fresh card and jotting down the proposed fix as briefly as you can. Then put that card away, out of sight, too!

In the interim, do some other work or planning or reading designed to establish a bit of space between yourself and the manuscript . . . and to let your poor, aching brain rest a little. This might be a great time to catch up with the neglected work in the garden, or to paint a bedroom, or even to start planning another, entirely different story. Or you might relax by reading some of those stories by others that you delayed reading during first draft for fear of unconscious imitation. Or perhaps you play tennis and golf, or like to fish, or belong to a sewing club. Any activity of this sort, especially if it has an aerobic exercise component, will rest you, reward you, distance you a bit, and refresh every part of you for the task that still remains ahead.

So give yourself a little break at this time. Meditate. Take in a movie. Ride a bike. Make love. Go to church. Bake a cake. Call a neglected friend for lunch (and don't talk writing!).

If you find thoughts of your story drifting through your mind, don't beat yourself up for failing to distance yourself; some preoccupation will be inevitable. But don't brood or worry, either. Just let the thought drift into your mind . . . and watch it drift right back out again. (Many writers find that they start thinking about an entirely different story at this point, perhaps that "inspiration" they had partway through the draft of this latest one. Those who discover such thoughts often begin to tinker mentally with the new idea, and that takes their mind away from that unmentionable "thing" in the bottom desk drawer.)

Perhaps, if you're still following my instructions carefully, you'll even want to go back and re-read one or more earlier chapters of this book, seeing if you might have missed something or glossed over an important point.

Whatever you do, work to think about anything but the project we've been so obsessed with for so long, here.

## TARGETING MARKETS

By this time, I hope you have a fairly good idea of the kind of magazine you hope to "hit" with your short story. We did some analysis of that kind in chapters three and five, if you'll remember. Now, the cooling-off period, is also a good time to pick up the latest copies of these publications, and perhaps some others you suspect might be similar, and give them some detailed study.

Since you have (like me) practically become a "card addict" by this time, you may wish to do some of this additional analysis in a form that allows you to fill out cards for each publication you examine for a second or third time.

Here are a few more points to consider about publications:

**Target audience as indicated by the cover.** Do you see a young, glamorous career girl or an older, wholesome young mother? Or perhaps a shaggy dude on a Harley?

**Hints from the table of contents.** How many fiction stories do you find? What percentage of the magazine is devoted to fiction? Do the story titles or contents blurbs (if any) hint about desired reader appeal?

**Titles and types of articles.** Again, what do titles or suggested contents say about probable reader age, content preference, income, other demographic data?

**Advertising.** Do you see ads mainly for household products? Clothing? Upscale electronic gear? All these things show what the magazine is holding out to advertisers as its target audience . . . and if the ads reflect a targeted age group or class of people, evidently the magazine is doing a good job at grabbing whatever audience it says it is seeking.

**The fiction in the issue.** Once before you read stories in a magazine as an assignment. You made notes on demographics, story length, setting and some other factors. Do that again now. In addition—and this may be far more important than you think—pick a few dozen paragraphs of copy out of the middle of two or three stories in the magazine, even if you have to do to more than one issue to find that many stories. Select your excerpts arbitrarily. If you could do it by putting the magazine on the wall and throwing a dart at it, so much the better.

Now carefully copy the chosen segment of each story until you have three or perhaps four pages typed on your typewriter or computer. Study how the typescript of the finished, published story generally compares with your own.

Most obvious, does the copy tend to *look like* the kind of manuscript you produce? If the published story has half of most pages raggedly blank because of short dialogue, what does that mean in terms of your story with full, fat paragraphs?

Or if the paragraphs of description or narration in the published story tend to average five lines in length, and you see that yours fill pages, what does *that* mean?

Study sentence lengths — count some words and then look at an earlier story of yours — not the one we've been working on here — and compare: Are your sentences the "right" length for this publication?

Examine word choice. Most word processing programs will make the simplest aspect of this task simpler yet. See if your spell-checker will tell you how many words are ten letters or less, how many fifteen to eighteen letters, let's say, and how many are longer than that? Or how many words are two syllables or less, how many three syllables, how many longer than that. If you find drastic differences between the copy you duplicated and your own work, something about your eventual market intentions has gone haywire.

It may sound like the dumbest exercise in the world, but I have had students whose eyes were truly opened by it. A comparison of appearance can be startling and instructive, because we don't see our copy on the printout page the way a reader will see it in a magazine. Our manuscript pages do not look like printed pages. The seemingly short paragraph on a page eight inches wide may look monstrously long when printed in a column less than two inches wide. Sometimes such obvious and simple physical comparisons can make you see things about your style, which may need changing, or your supposed target magazine, which may not be "your meat" after all.

## RECORDING YOUR OBSERVATIONS

Anything you notice in any of this analytical work should be jotted on cards, as stated above, and perhaps transposed to a page of your journal as a more permanent record.

And also, while you are cooling off, it's a great time to make one or more longer entries in your journal. Record how you're feeling about the current project — not revision notes or anything like that, you understand, but how you *feel* — excited or tired or discouraged or elated or whatever. Write down what you have learned thus far through the project.

Finally, write a few paragraphs in your journal about what you see as positive about this story. Where do you steadfastly believe you can — and will — sell this story? How will the next story be even better? In what ways are you a better writer than you were a month or two ago? How is it going to feel when you have achieved the success that is now within your reach, given hard work, intelligent planning, and perhaps a gift from your God?

Please don't do any of this suggested work in a driven or compulsive manner! It would be better to do little or none of it than to drive yourself into further fatigue. This is a sort of working vacation.

When you have put in a week or more doing the kind of work suggested in this brief chapter, perhaps you will have gone through a cooling-off period sufficient to let you move on to the rest of your revision process. But leave the manuscript in the drawer for just a little while . . . until you have begun chapter sixteen.

## SUMMARY

Revision of a manuscript is aided if the writer allows for a cooling-off period before tackling most of the work. That's because no writer ever sees her work with total clarity, and in the first days and weeks after creating a rough draft, it is virtually impossible to see with any degree of objectivity.

Factual repairs or the cleaning up of plot odds and ends, for example, may be made at once. But the rest of revision should wait a week or more.

During this time, the writer should think about other things and do other things that are likely to be refreshing. Some healthy outdoor or other aerobic exercise is especially beneficial.

During this time, further market research can be done in a fairly organized way. "Organized," however, does not mean compulsive.

# DEVICES: FLASHBACK, DIALOGUE, VOICE

While you're letting your copy cool a bit, you might like to read this section in search of some general answers to questions often asked at writers conferences. These questions usually involve writing devices, and almost always grow out of the questioner's tangle with a writing problem involving them. While we can't possibly answer all such questions that might have come into your mind while you were writing the first draft, we can take a shot at a few of the most common . . . and hope something in the answers will solve or clarify something that's been bothering you, too.

## FLASHBACK

The writer's device that is almost universally asked about during conferences or classes is the flashback. Someone invariably asks, "Should I use flashback?"

The answer is: maybe.

An elaboration is: Please stop worrying about nonessentials.

You have worked through the essentials of short-story writing as you worked your way through this book. "Flashback" is one of those additional elements of fiction that isn't in the mainstream of a writer's concerns. If she needs one, she'll produce one. If she doesn't, she won't. She doesn't fret about it.

But perhaps you're that rarest of writers, one who either doesn't worry about the use of flashback or even know exactly what it is. In that case, let's take a quick look at the device and make some observations.

Flashback, in its purest definition, is the playing of a story event onstage in the story "now" — as if it were taking place in the present — even though it really took place earlier, probably before the story started on page one.

For example, Penelope is haunted by a vicious fight she once had with her father. During her present story, which is about her attempt to reconcile with her errant husband, she remembers the violent scene with her father. *Perhaps* the writer decides that this old scene was so compelling and central to the present story that he must play it onstage now, for all its possible impact on the reader. And so he stops the present action and flashes back to play the old event, moment by moment, in all its awful glory.

In this example, please note that I attempted to *justify* the use of a flashback by saying that the writer decided that the old scene was not only compelling, but *central to the present story*. Both tests must be passed before a writer should even consider the possible use of a flashback. Just because you can use one, you don't have to — and probably shouldn't in a vast majority of cases.

I have read student stories, for example, in which the slightest little past event was dragged into the present action and presented as a full-blown flashback when it had no central relevance to the present story and could just as easily have been summarized in a sentence — or even forgotten about altogether. I asked a student about this once and she told me, "I just felt like I ought to have a flashback in there somewhere."

Such decisions come from obsession with such devices as flashback. They are almost always errant.

You already know that the background of major characters must be worked out carefully, and that many past events probably have been thought through before you elected to start the story past the time when they took place. All this material might be made the stuff of flashback, but it is not flashback *per se*. This kind of stuff that happened before page one is called *backstory*. Every story has a load of author-imagined backstory, even if 99 percent of it is never told in the manuscript itself. So backstory is good and universal and needed, so long as you have the wisdom to recognize that it is *not* flashback in itself — and just because you know backstory is no justification for cramming it into your story as a flashback.

How, then, do you get the story of old events into your story present? Very simply, you allow your viewpoint character to ruminate about them, or you have two characters discuss them, or you slip them in through some trick such as an old newspaper clipping or letter.

In all such cases, make the rumination or discussion or whatever as short as possible — then get on with the present.

Before you do any of these things, however, look hard at your story and ask yourself how much of the backstory *really* has to be told in the present story. Remember that the reader doesn't give a hoot about whatever history you have invented, unless it impinges directly on the present action, the motives and actions of the characters onstage now. You might, for example, have concocted a magnificent and colorful history for that little southern town you're using as setting in this story. But if the history doesn't really affect the present action, you have to leave out almost all of it.

However, if you decide that some backstory detail simply must be presented, search for the method of presentation that will allow the maximum in brevity. And trust that when the rare situation comes along which demands a true flashback, you'll sense it — and write it as a short scene just like any other scene in your story.

## DIALOGUE

It may surprise you to see dialogue listed among fiction devices. As discussed in our first Time Out, among other places, dialogue is an integral part of most short stories; it can illuminate character, advance the plot and even inform the reader of events, if handled carefully enough.

Dialogue, however, has other functions in the short story, and there are dialogue devices that might be helpful to the developing writer hitherto unfamiliar with them. In most modern short fiction, dialogue is among the fastest-reading elements of the story: Characters speak in clipped tones and often in sentence fragments. If you were to retype a page or two of this dialogue, you would notice that the right half of the page was mostly empty, the very short dialogue statements ending so abruptly on most lines that they were not filled to the margin. Further, you might notice that dialogue tends to appear at a point in the story where maximum confrontation or tension was evident — at the high moments.

For both reasons—brevity and tension—dialogue is speedy. The reader's eye flies along and perhaps his breath becomes ragged with worry. There are usually serious issues at stake when there is story dialogue, and the short sentences and short paragraphs lend themselves to a skimming movement by the reader's eye.

To put all this in the form of a lesson that a writer might apply, consider it this way: Dialogue, because it is swift, can be used as a speed-control device in your story; if you feel the story is moving too slowly, you can create a dialogue transaction that ought to speed things up; conversely, if you fear your story is rushing along too quickly, perhaps you need to look for places where dialogue transactions might be changed into slower-moving character thought. There are writers, of course, who favor lengthy speeches by their characters. In such situations, dialogue might even slow down a story. But, as stated before, *most* modern dialogue reads quickly.

It could be beneficial for every writer to study her own dialogue now and then, and try to judge how fast it is when compared with other elements of the same story. As discussed in our first Time Out section, straight narration is probably the fastest-moving mode of discourse available to us. But dialogue may well be second. Does your dialogue speed along when there is story tension? And are you handling story conversation with a full awareness of its utility as a speed-control device?

In addition to its usefulness as a device for control of story speed, however, story talk has other useful qualities. Another of these is its use as a color device.

Dialogue today is seldom acceptable if it too closely mimics regional or ethnic dialect. As stated earlier, the charge of some kind of bigotry or bias is too often lodged against the writer, no matter how innocent and well meaning she might be. But dialogue can still be used to suggest regional color or individual background if it is handled with a light hand.

It is still quite acceptable, for example, to indicate a southern upbringing by allowing a character to say "y'all" in a story—provided you avoid overkill. If you were to add dialogue eccentricities such as "fanger" for "finger," "chillun" for "children," and "vittles" (or victuals) for food, then you might be accused of going too far, making the speakers sound ignorant. In a similar way, you might hint at the color of an Italian background by allowing a character to talk about his love for pasta with pesto sauce, and sip a glass of homemade red wine. But if you started trying to mimic an imagined Italian accent, or had a character refer to his homemade wine as "Dago red"—as Italian friends of mine often do—you would again be accused of pushing a good thing too far.

In strict moderation, then, dialogue may be useful to indicate color of region or ethnic background. But it is a very dangerous technique.

Less dangerous, perhaps, is use of dialogue *content* rather than accent or wordage to introduce local color into a story. In a story set in Missouri along the Mississippi River, for example, characters might refer to "the river" as a place for a picnic, even if the picnic scene never shows up in the story. Or they might comment that a rainstorm would raise the level of the river . . . or they might mention that state workers were repairing a bridge over the river. Or a character might even speak of lying in the stillness of the night and hearing the distant murmur of water.

Another example might be a story set in a big city. The color of the city environment could easily be shown by having one character briefly talk with another about the sounds of the streets, like this:

> "It's always so loud," Bill said.
>
> "Loud?" Tom repeated, puzzled.
>
> "The constant roar of the traffic. Always distant sirens— another accident, another crime. It makes me nervous."
>
> Tom paused and cocked his head, listening. "Yes," he said finally. "I guess you get used to it."

You may notice as you scan this brief example that the use of the dialogue to indicate local color—in this case the characteristic roar of city traffic—is not thrown into the tale haphazardly or for its own sake alone. The brief conversation also tells the reader how tense Bill feels, and it clearly demonstrates one sharp difference between Bill and Tom, evidently a city dweller so accustomed to his environment that he doesn't hear the noise at all. This is the way the short story writer will usually use the device of dialogue for color: She will make it do double or triple duty, so that she does not use up precious words for any single purpose.

Such uses of dialogue to introduce a character awareness of story setting is often useful. Its potential is, unfortunately, rarely recognized. During the later stages of your story revision, you may wish to be alert to possibilities for having characters talk *briefly* about some aspect of the color around the action; the reader's ability to imagine the setting could well be enhanced.

Another way dialogue can be used to accomplish further ends in a short story is as an insight device. Again, it's a dangerous technique if carried too far, or if it becomes an obvious crutch for a writer who repeatedly uses it, proving she doesn't know any other way of getting certain information into the story. But it will solve real problems for you if done correctly, and in moderation.

For example, when you are in the viewpoint of character A, and desperately need to let the reader know what's going on inside the mind of character B, you might be tempted to switch viewpoints. But as already discussed, such changes in viewpoint may confuse the reader or stop the story, at least temporarily. What, then, to do? You might try (a) having the nonviewpoint character state directly what's on her mind, or (b) having the viewpoint character acutely notice something apparently hidden behind what was just said by the nonviewpoint character. That explanation reads like a mouthful. Yet the technique of dialogue as an insight device is really quite simple. Illustrations will help you see exactly what it entails.

Assume for a moment that you have Bill and Tom, onstage again. You are in Bill's viewpoint. But you believe it is mandatory that the reader know Tom is both worried—and lying to his friend, or holding back some unknown information.

The simplest solution might be to change to Tom's viewpoint, but we are aware of the dangers of that. So we use dialogue as insight device, something like the following:

> Bill studied his friend's face. *[Establishes Bill as the viewpoint character.]* He could see the uncharacteristic worry lines around Tom's eyes. "What's bothering you?" he asked.
> "Nothing," Tom snapped.
> "What are you holding back?" Bill insisted. . . .

Thus, in a very brief segment, viewpoint character Bill's observations and dialogue tell the reader how worried Tom is, and that he is holding something back.

Suppose, on the other hand, you needed to show the reader that Tom was lying. Do you see how simply you might have Tom say something that Bill *knew* was untrue, then have Bill accuse him of lying, then have Tom angrily deny it—and say something else that Bill could instantly suspect was also a lie?

You may even wish to practice the technique by writing this brief dialogue transaction.

It's a valuable device. Just be sure, however, that you use it sparingly, and do *not* fall into the trap of using dialogue as speech-making, wherein one character starts lecturing another just for your authorial convenience. It would *not* be acceptable, in other words, to write a dialogue transaction like the following:

"What's wrong?" Bill asked.

"I'm worried sick," Tom replied. "Last night's events kept me awake without a wink. I have a headache. Now I have some further information I might give you, but I'm not going to tell you about it. You don't need to know. If you ask about it, I'm going to lie to you because. . . ."

You can see how obvious and amateurish this is. Also, to enforce the definition of dialogue that we've been using throughout this book, this might not even be dialogue at all; it's speech-making.

The study of published story dialogue can become a part of the writer's lifelong quest for self-improvement. No two writers handle dialogue in precisely the same way. One may be so terse as to seem telegraphic, while another may drop in a few long and leisurely sentences now and again to give the impression of laziness. One writer may use dialogue to indicate color, another to tell out-of-viewpoint thoughts or feelings. The wise student writer will be alert for all such variations from a predictable norm in the handling of dialogue, and will consider whether something learned here can be applied to her own ongoing work.

## VOICE

All good writers have a "voice," a typical combination of story content, theme and language that gives their work a felicitous feeling or tone or unspoken sound. The voice of Poe is not that of Updike. The voice of Hemingway is far from the voice of Daphne du Maurier. When a writer is writing at top form, this feeling of the totality of the story and its language works its own magic to make the impact on the reader greater than any of its constituents.

Most of us are brought to writing in the first place partly because we come upon a writer whose style and voice so impress us that we want to emulate them. Most of us begin writing by struggling to develop our own writing style, and out of the style a personal voice.

Unfortunately, a writer's characteristic voice is one of the last things that develops, something that just seems to happen. Struggling to find an individual voice is a little like trying to remember a name that's tantalizingly close to consciousness, but that keeps eluding you: The harder and more directly you look at the problem, the easier the answer slides away. Only when you think about something else does the answer come unbidden.

Nevertheless, since so many writers remain preoccupied with development of a voice, a few general observations should be made on the subject.

First of all, a writer's voice stems primarily from her choice of vocabulary, her syntax and her rhythms. Let's look briefly at these aspects.

If you always tend to search for the biggest word, for example, your voice may become that of a university professor, intent on "publish or perish," and seeking to impress his colleagues out there with his dry erudition and "scientific" approach to his research and writing. On the other hand, if you are writing a children's book, you may consciously select a much simpler and more basic vocabulary, so that your story in this case has the voice of a seven-year-old. Word choice — complex or simple, basic or abstract — can go far toward helping to establish voice.

It may be, too, that something in your own ethnic or regional derivation will affect your voice in a subtle way. A southern writer, for example, might thoughtlessly refer to a noon meal as "dinner," while a northerner would use that term only for the evening meal. Another writer might have a person kneeling to eat her lunch at a picnic, while some other writer, from a Roman Catholic background, could not conceive of using the word "kneeling" in any context but that of the church.

Of such subtle word choices is "voice" developed.

Syntax, too, plays a part. Do you tend to write in simple, declarative sentences, or perhaps in rolling, sonorous complex constructions? Do you tend to write in short sentences, or do you often link independent clauses with coordinating conjunctions? Are your paragraphs classically constructed with frequent topic sentences and logical development, point by point, or are they written in journalistic style, with short paragraphs that link in the pattern of the traditional newspaper inverted pyramid? Do you sometimes use sentence fragments for effect, or is every sentence complete? Is the average length of your sentences in the neighborhood of twelve to twenty words, or do you find many sentences that run longer than fifty? All such factors can and do enter into what becomes your voice.

Consider, too, the rhythms and cadences of your finished prose. To refer again to two writers mentioned earlier, the rhythm of Ernest Hemingway is quick, sharp, staccato, brittle. The rhythm of Daphne du Maurier is much more lengthy, poetic, evocative, rolling, almost wavelike. While the typical modern short story tends to be simple, direct and sparse, differences of rhythm do exist. Perhaps a study of your own style in this regard — even to quietly reading some of your pages aloud with no one else present — could give you an insight as to your own developing voice.

Now, I realize that we have gotten into very deep water with this discussion of voice, but perhaps an additional observation or two should be made. One of these has to do with the plot content of your story and how this can have a direct impact on your voice.

Content can affect voice. It is hard to imagine, for example, that a hard-boiled detective story could be told in the same authorial voice that would be used to narrate an idyllic youthful romance. People who write for magazines like *Penthouse* do not have the voice of those who write for something like the old *True Detective*, and neither has a voice that would fit gently into a magazine like *Good Housekeeping*. Why? Simply because the writers are writing about different subject matter, and from different perspectives. Their content reflects their perspective and has a direct impact on how they write.

Look, for example, at the stories in a current issue of a crime-fiction magazine and a story in a magazine directed toward young women. The content will be different. You will also immediately note the stylistic differences that contribute to vastly differing tones.

Voice will not only be affected by content, but voice to some degree can be controlled at the author's will, depending on what the content happens to be. A writer like Phyllis Whitney, for example, has one voice in her adult mysteries and a somewhat different voice in the books she writes for younger readers. Sometimes a writer will develop a certain voice while writing one kind of story, then later write another kind of story; if she maintains the same voice in the second story, she may write with a tone and emphasis that does not fit the new subject matter.

How do you analyze your own voice? As stated, reading aloud

may help. Formal analysis may also be of assistance. A careful analytical study of writers competing in the same marketplace — with the same kinds of stories that you now wish to write — may reveal differences of voice. This is a subtle matter, and may not come easily.

Finally, let's be aware of authorial tone and voice, and try to develop our writing in such a way that our own voice can emerge. But let's not "get bent out of shape" over it. A writer's voice *will* emerge is she strives to write in a style consistent with her content — and if she strives always for simplicity and directness.

If you strive for simplicity and directness in your writing style — and, paradoxically, *don't search actively* for a voice all of your own — then one will inevitably develop over time. Something that is uniquely you will grow out of the simple beginnings. It's only when you look directly at the matter that you can't get it in focus. It's only when you thrash around, trying all sorts of styles, that you never seem to develop one you can truly call yours and yours alone.

Your voice may vary from time to time, from story to story, and from intended audience to intended audience. But there will be a bedrock foundation beneath it that is unchanging. This can only come from years of work and an unblinking scrutiny of how best to tell the story, while letting nothing so esoteric or abstract as "voice" enter your mind.

*Chapter Sixteen*

# Revising Your Copy, Part II

---

PROGRESS CHECK:

✔ *Have you allowed at least a week for cooling off?*

✔ *Have you perhaps done some further analysis of some of your target publications?*

✔ *Have you made observations in your journal?*

---

A fter allowing for a cooling-off period and putting some small distance between yourself and your new manuscript, you're ready for the work that can be the most bothersome but most rewarding of all: final revision. Here is where we reach "make or break" time, the work that separates the men from the boys, the women from the girls, the pros from the amateurs. It's an exciting time, and I congratulate you for reaching it.

Now let's go to work and make it all come together.

This is the time when you finally get to dig into that bottom desk drawer and pull out the manuscript. But do you grab a red pencil and start a furious editing job at once? No. We'll take revision like we've taken everything else, one step at a time, and in a sequence designed for maximum efficiency and benefit.

## PHASE I—A CASUAL READING

Of course no one in the world could really give their fresh, new manuscript a truly "casual" reading at this point! But that's what we aim for first, trying as best we can to trick ourselves into seeing the story as others will see it.

In chapter fifteen we discussed most of the reasons we can't ever do a totally "cold" reading, like other readers will do. We looked, too, at some of the pitfalls resulting from our own closeness to the manuscript. That, you'll remember, is why we enforced a brief vacation from the manuscript.

Now, before you get totally engrossed in the manuscript once again, you should try to see it as cooly and casually as possible. But reading it now with a red pencil in your hand is a writer's or editor's job, not that of a fresh reader. So how do you get yourself to read as if you had never read the story before?

Set aside a time when you feel reasonably confident that the house or apartment will be quiet, and that you won't be disturbed. If necessary, tell your family that you need an hour or two of solitude. If you have a telephone answering machine, turn it on and vow to let it do the answering for the next little while.

Carry the manuscript out of your work office and into the living room, or wherever you characteristically relax or read for the fun of it. Put some quiet music on the stereo if you like; just make sure it won't actively engage your attention. Turn on a light over your favorite chair, or arrange the draperies for reading. If you usually drink coffee or tea when reading for pleasure, have some coffee or tea.

What we're trying to do here, you see, is create an atmosphere as *unlike* your work environment and as *like* your pleasure-reading situation as we can. Sit down, relax, close your eyes. Breathe slowly. Be aware of your breathing. Perhaps you will be conscious of your own heartbeat, or sounds from out on the street. If thoughts fill your mind, let them drift across your consciousness without worrying about them. Relax your hands and arms, your feet and legs, your back and the heavy muscles across your shoulders. Let some time pass . . . perhaps five minutes, perhaps a bit more.

When you are ready to come back to the here and now, let your eyes open slowly. Yawn, if you feel like it. Gently stretch.

Now—and only now—you may pick up your manuscript and begin to read it at your normal reading pace, whatever that may be. Look for *nothing in particular* as your read. Just enjoy without being critical.

If you notice an error or weak spot or inconsistency, just read right on and don't worry about it.

Once you have finished this reading, let the pages rest again on your lap or the arm of the chair or sofa, lean back, and think about what you have experienced in reading the story. Were there parts you liked very much? Were you able to see the general tone and flow of the story better than ever before? Congratulate yourself.

After relaxing a few more minutes, perhaps, you have accomplished the all-important revision Phase I, that of seeing your story more clearly from beginning to end. You are ready for the next steps, which should begin right away.

## PHASE II—STRUCTURAL REVISION PLANNING

It's a high-falutin' phrase, that "structural revision planning." All it really means is the process whereby you carry your story back to your desk, and glance over it one more time, then make notes for any serious revisions you might have decided will be necessary.

You may have already made some revision notes—changing the names of characters, etc.—even as you wrote the first draft, or immediately thereafter. Now, at this later stage, you may have detected other internal inconsistencies, or your reading after a cooling-off period may have helped you detect some flaw in story timing, a flat spot that might be more dramatic, or something of that nature. Now is the time to handle these new revision chores in one of two ways:

1. You may choose to write the corrections in the margins or between the lines of the existing manuscript, or you may reopen your computer file and actually type in the revisions you have noted.

2. Or you may jot notes about intended revisions on more of your file cards, then simply stack them up with identifying manuscript page numbers, or stick them onto the pages due a fix.

In either case, please note that we still aren't shooting for a final, letter-perfect manuscript. However you note or insert the corrections to characters, plot, setting or pacing, you don't have to worry about neatness. Just note them in whatever way feels best to you.

This process may sound simple but sometimes it's difficult. A change in a story has a rippling or domino effect down through all the rest of the pages. I once changed the sex of the viewpoint character from male to female at this point, for example, after making a serious error in all the prior planning; the new character's problem was the same, but habits, manner of dress, friends and even characteristic preoccupations changed all the way through the story as a result of what might at first blush appear to be a simple enough change.

However long it may take you to perform these repairs, by all means take that time and do so now, before moving on.

## PHASE III — SYNTAX ANALYSIS

Another fancy term! It means that you have now reached the stage in your revision where you check, line by line and word by word, how your writing style stacks up.

This may seem a relatively minor step to be taking at this stage of revision. There are writers who maintain that a few misspelled words or errors of grammar don't make much difference. I had a writing teacher who used to growl, "Don't worry about that stuff; that's what they've got editors to fix; you just tell a good story!"

It might have been valid advice in its day, but it is no longer true. Editors in the publishing industry today are universally harried, worried and badly overworked. They simply cannot afford to buy a story if they see it is going to take hours correcting stupid mechanical errors that no writer with pride would have submitted in the first place.

So here you're "cleaning up your act" in terms of spelling, grammar and syntax — and you'd better be careful doing it!

Some word processing programs can help you. There are spell-checkers, dictionaries, thesauruses and elaborate programs to check your grammar. If you have some of these and want to run them at this point, fine. But please remember that no such program can catch everything that may be wrong.

You may have typed, "It was not to easy," for example, when obviously you meant to write, "It was not too easy." No spell-checker is going to flag that for you. Or you might have typed, "A black cat raced down the street at sixty-five miles per hour" when in reality you meant, "A black *car* raced down the street at sixty-five miles per hour." The spell-checker doesn't know what you meant. It determines if the word exists, and, if it does, whether it seems to be spelled correctly. So the spell-checker will blithely let that "black cat" race on down the street at sixty-five.

Grammar programs, in my limited experience, are even worse. Most of them are written to flag such "errors" as sentence fragments, comma faults, contact clauses, and the like. Yet you may *want* to write several hard-hitting sentence fragments during a tense scene, as a stylistic way of making the scene seem even more brittle and dramatic. Or to show the close relationship between two causal factors, you may intentionally connect two independent clauses without the usual coordinating conjunction — thus creating a comma fault — again for desired effect.

Such programs are good at helping a nonwriting writer create clear, pedestrian, predictable prose. There's nothing wrong with that. But your style and story situation may demand so many deviations from the norm that all you accomplish in running a grammar-checker is irritation.

None of this means that you should be careless with grammar or spelling, or say something like, "That just happens to be my style." You must know when a rule applies, and when (for a very specific reason) you might choose to violate a rule. If you are wobbly on grammar, now is the time to stop everything and bone up. There are night classes that offer grammar and basic writing. A trip to your local bookstore will reveal a shelf of easy-to-read books on the subject. If you are not sure, at least review a little!

Having done so, turn back to your manuscript once more with a red pencil or ballpoint in hand. Read carefully. Search out typographical errors, grammar problems, spelling uncertainties. Make these corrections right now, even though you may be marking on a very messy manuscript. You might forget them later.

Read carefully, too, to make sure that what you wrote was what you really meant. Perhaps you wrote that it was a "glum day" when you meant that it was a gray and depressing day; *people* are glum. Or perhaps you can find some abominations like misplaced modifiers or dangling participles, things like the following:

Running, he blew his nose. (I think you meant his nose was running, which was why he blew it. But that's not what was written.) *Or* —

Red-faced, they saw him run across the finish line. (I think the author meant that the runner was red-faced, but again. . . .) *Or* —

Dank and dreary, with no overhead light, his flashlight dimmed as he went down the steps. (I don't think I'll even comment on that one.)

Look, too, for "in" phrases or common jargon that will quickly appeared dated, and may already look ignorant. A few years ago, everything was said to be a "paradigm" of something else. Then we went into—and sadly remain in—the age of "hopefully." At this writing, a lot of people seem to be talking about how the weather can *impact* on a sports event, or a bad tooth can *impact* on one's outlook, or whatever.

The moral: Write straight copy, not jargon. It will stand up better over the years—and might even please an editor whose teeth are ground to powder from reading such atrocities.

Look for overwriting—flowery phrases or the use of ten words when one or two would do.

Take out those pages you copied earlier from a publication you desired to "hit." Count words in the average sentence, if you didn't do so earlier, and then establish a best estimate of the number of words in the average paragraph. Then do the same analysis for a few pages of your own manuscript copy. Do they appear to be in the same stylistic ballpark? If not, do you intend to change your copy or look for a different magazine that may publish stuff more in your natural style?

Select at least three random pages of your story, say pages 3, 5 and 8, or any three that are not in sequence or all of the same kind (all pages of dialogue, for example, or all pages of narration). Count the number of words in all the sentences. You should find a pleasing variety, from a few very short ones (three to six words) to a few that might be rated quite long (25 to 50 words).

If you find that all your sentences tend to be very short, it might mean that your style is jerky and very fast. This may be all right in an action story, but could be deadly in a more thoughtful study of character. Conversely, if you are trying to write dynamite action, and find that your average sentence length is 30 words, you are in big trouble; such long sentences tend to slow everything down.

Look for all words of three syllables or longer. Count the number of letters in all the words on at least three pages. Words of three syllables or more should be few and far between. Most long words belong in academic journals, not in popular fiction.

(If you are on an adequate word processing program, perhaps you can do this entire part of your story analysis through access to something like a History Screen.)

Everything you find questionable should be fixed in red pencil or pen *now*, before you move on to heavier matters.

## PHASE IV—TACTICAL ANALYSIS

Here we get into heavy-duty final checking of the story from as many practical aspects as we can think of. We may go through the story a dozen or more times, because we can't look for everything at once.

If the manuscript has gotten messy, you may want to keyboard in all corrections to date, and print out fresh copy.

At any rate, here we go on the *almost*-final checking.

Some writers try to do all the following checks on the computer or word processor, staring at the screen as they go. You may have noticed that I seldom suggest working on-screen, and that's because of a personal hang-up: I can't *see* some mistakes and problems on-screen. I need pages in front of me.

Some writers also work with pages, but stop and write in every change or correction as they go along. Others make notes for things to be fixed later, often using file cards like yours. My own system involves notes in the margins, paste-ins, cards, and everything but my rosary beads. However you choose to do the following analytic work, just be sure you do it in what is for you a workable, systematic fashion.

To help make this as systematic as possible, a number of writers I've known over the years developed their own personal checklist for this revision phase. You may start with the following list, and plan to add to it as you discover other aspects you will always want to check in future work.

This is a starter, in other words, not an all-inclusive checklist.

Ask yourself the following questions, and check the following aspects.

## Background

Is there any aspect of this work, either in terms of factual research or the imagined background of a character, that needs further study or analysis? (Look for any spot where you might have tried to slip by on inadequate factual information. Look for any character who seems to come from nowhere and have no history at all.)

Look at the motives of your major characters. Have you included sufficient information about their past lives, their dreams and aspirations, to make it credible that they would want what they want here, and act as they act? Have you made sure to give them background experience that qualifies them to do what may need to be done in the story? (For example, if the hero must trek out of a wilderness, have you made sure to mention that he once went to a wilderness survival school?)

Have the characters *stated* their intentions and problems in the story? Do we hear them say who and what they are, based on where they came from? Have we provided some introspection for the most important characters so we can share their thoughts and emotions, and see how they are children of their background in a believable way?

## Characters

Look at your character names. Remembering that a name can be a tag, do the names generally fit the people?

Are the names sufficiently varied? Have you perhaps gotten onto a "-ham" name kick and inadvertently named characters Framing-*ham* and Bucking*ham* and Cunning*ham*? Or on an unrealized pre-occupation where names may look different, but accidentally sound alike, such as John and Sean and Don and Juan? Or Jerry and Terry and Barry and Mary? The unconscious does funny things some-times. This sort of error with similar names is extremely common, and must be checked at this point to avoid reader confusion.

Are your major characters bigger than life? Go through the story and note the specific passages that identify them the most vividly — in the most striking way. Are there enough of these? Are you sure you haven't fallen into the trap of writing about average people in average situations? That can be deadly dull.

What is the self-concept of each major character? Have you clearly defined this on a card, as well as in the story? Can you find the character uttering his or her self-concept in statements such as, "I'm the kind of person who . . . ," or whatever? Do your characters act in terms of their self-concept? For example, does the woman who sees herself as a shy person consistently act shy in the story, and perhaps even worry about it? Do characters' occupations, hob-bies and surroundings complement their self-concepts? Do their story goals somehow relate to their self-concepts?

What is the essential personality trait of each character? What tags have you devised to show and demonstrate this trait? Have you been careful to show the tag more than once, to make sure the reader picks up on it?

Do your characters speak realistically to one another? Does their speech appear to be like some of the interesting real-life speech you have recorded on observation cards? Do the characters interrupt one another, talk at cross-purposes, repeat key words sometimes, engage in brisk conversation? Are you sure you aren't having your story people make speeches at one another?

Have you provided a brief physical description of each character to help the reader visualize them?

Do the major characters contrast with one another—something as simple, perhaps, as a tall character being contrasted with a short one, or perhaps a stingy character being cast against a foil character who is generous with everyone?

Are you absolutely sure that you and the characters—and the reader—all know what's troubling the major characters, what they want?

## Viewpoint

Read carefully through your copy, remembering who the viewpoint character is at all times. Look for failures in viewpoint, or confusion about viewpoint. Are you sure that what you're describing can be experienced by the viewpoint character at this moment? Have you perhaps erred by telling the reader what the expression is on the viewpoint character's face, when in fact the viewpoint character can't *see* his own expression? Are you sure you have not gotten directly into someone else's thoughts, or allowed the viewpoint character to know something she couldn't realistically know?

If you changed viewpoint in your story, are you sure the change was absolutely mandatory, and not just a weak contrivance to make life easier for you? Remember that every viewpoint change risks losing the reader . . . diluting the suspense.

Have you been sure to include some direct statements of what the viewpoint character senses, thinks and feels—and none of anyone else?

Is the viewpoint character the most interesting in the story? The one whose problem or goal lies at the heart of the story question?

Is he or she active? Trying? Moving? Changing?

Is the viewpoint character someone you could like in real life? Understand?

Are you sure you haven't fallen into the trap of making the viewpoint character a passive observer?

Do you need to improve the viewpoint character in any way, perhaps by adding to her problems or emotional responses?

## Plot and Structure

What is the story question?

Does the story question become clear very early in the story?

Does the story focus throughout on the story question?

Does the ending answer the story question?

How many scenes in your story?

How many sequels?

Can you identify any one of either that might be cut with no harm to the story?

Do scenes lead logically to sequels, and sequels motivate the scenes that follow them?

Does each scene open with a stated short-term goal that can be seen as a stepping stone to the story goal, or an attempt to solve the story problem?

Does each scene contain conflict (preferably) or at least serious adversity?

Are your scene-ending disasters organic?

Is each disaster of the kind that makes life more complex or bleak for the viewpoint character? Is he farther than ever behind the eight ball as a result of just having tried to accomplish something?

Do your sequels look into the character's head and heart alike? That is, are you sure you have portrayed both thoughts and emotions of the viewpoint character in those sequels you elected to "play" for the reader?

Comparing your story at this point with the cards or block diagram you prepared earlier, do you see serious deviations from the plan? If so, why did you deviate? Are you convinced the deviation from the plan was wise, and not a momentary creative insanity?

Have you introduced any secondary problems or characters that really only confuse the basic story issues? Have you at any point played a discussion or struggle or introspection that is clearly irrelevant to what the story is supposed to be about?

Is your ending of the type where something—anything—*happens*? Have you avoided the dreaded story-ending lecture or sermon, wherein the author tries to save the day by telling the reader what it was supposed to mean . . . and how the reader is supposed to feel about it?

## Miscellaneous

Could any outside reader identify any real people in your story? Is there any chance you have too closely copied a real person who might be offended . . . or (worse) even file a lawsuit? Remember that fiction characters are not real-life characters, although the idea for the character may have started with a real person, or with several drawn in composite. Your story characters must be bigger than life.

If you have "jumped off" from some real-life situation as a basis for your story, are you sure you have changed real elements substantially to avoid hurting some real person or causing a lawsuit?

Watch for signs of "fine writing" — poetic flights or long, colorful descriptions of static situations or places. They're sure to slow or kill your story's progress, and should be eliminated.

## A FINAL PRINTOUT

Having checked your copy for all the items above, and any others that may have come to mind, you may wish to go back to a very early journal assignment and check what you saw then as your greatest strengths and greatest weaknesses as a writer. You may want to ask yourself now whether you feel the story takes full advantage of your perceived strengths. And you may want to scan the typescript once more to watch for signs of whatever you considered (and may still consider) your gravest weakness.

Having done this, it is a good idea to let the manuscript cool for a day or two, at least. Then it's time to make any corrections you haven't made earlier, make a final file, and print out the completed manuscript.

Look at it, page by page. Make sure there are no awkward "widow lines" — a single word atop a page finishing a previous-page paragraph, for example — or anything else that may have occurred typographically without your awareness. Sometimes we spot too many words underlined for emphasis at this point, or see several paragraphs in a row beginning with the same phrase or word. Anything like this that you find — fix.

◆ ◆ ◆

Finally, a word about an issue that often worries writers: protection of your ideas from theft. This is an issue that worries new writers far more than necessary. First, commercial editors are looking for finished copy, not ideas. There are always a zillion story ideas floating around. It's the execution of the idea that sells the story, not the idea itself.

Furthermore, the current copyright law states that copyright protection — the force of the federal government — *invests in the act of creation itself*. This simply means that you are protected from the moment you type or print out your page.

Therefore, the most you need to do is type a "Copyright, (year), (your name)" somewhere atop the first page—and even that simply is not necessary. You are already protected just by the fact that you wrote the story. I have known writers who mailed themselves a copy of the finished script, then filed away that postmarked and dated envelope, unopened of course. If doing something like that would make you feel better, go ahead. I have not yet ever heard of anyone having to use such a device in a case of alleged plagiarism.

And now are you ready to mail off your story? The story is now ready, I suspect. And you may already have a precise idea of where you want to send it. In that case, by all means put it in the mail.

If you have any doubts about markets or submissions, however, you may wish to skim the next chapter. It's likely the information there will be a review for you, because it's basic stuff. But maybe you'll pick up a pointer.

One more observation: A young writer I knew was asked when she knew she was truly finished fine-tuning her story revision. She replied, "When I am so sick of it that every word starts to look stupid, all my critical facilities are shot, and I just simply can't go on with it any longer."

This was real wisdom. You revise until you can't stand to do it any more, or have no reason for revising except crippling self-doubt. Every writer, I think, reaches a revision point where she simply *hates* everything about the story. Don't get discouraged if this happens to you; it just means you've probably revised sufficiently.

## SUMMARY

Manuscript revision is a multiple-stage process in which the writer looks first for one set of factors, and only later for another. While no writer can ever see her copy as cooly as can an outside reader, a brief cooling-off period helps her begin revision as critically as possible.

A "casual reading"—no pencil or notepad in hand—often lets you see the flow and feel of the story in a way you never can while working on the pieces.

Early detected major problems should be addressed in order, but constant reprinting or retyping of the manuscript is not necessary. Stylistic matters, including even such basics as spelling, form a revision step all of their own.

Devising a checklist for a final run-through of the draft is a good idea. This chapter contained a short one.

Note: As a convenience, a more detailed checklist, essentially covering all the steps and processes discussed in our hands-on approach to short story writing, appears as an appendix in this volume.

*Chapter Seventeen*

# Honing Your Marketing Skills

---

PROGRESS CHECK:

✔ *Is your story finished and on the desk?*

✔ *Are you continuing to observe real-life people in search of new characters and ideas?*

✔ *Have you made a journal entry or two in recent days, recording such items as how you feel about finishing this story . . . and perhaps what you think you would like to write next?*

✔ *Are you thinking about where to send this story?*

---

The planning is over, the creation is over, and now the revision is finished. It's time to think about sending this story out, and that's mainly what we'll look at, very briefly, in this chapter.

There is, however, something else you also need to be thinking about, as reflected in the "Progress Check" immediately above.

That's what you plan to write next.

There are several reasons why you should be thinking about that, and maybe already gearing up to do it all again . . . and again.

In the first place, whether you fully realize it or not, your ongoing work through the story you've done has smoothed your creative machinery — oiled up your imagination and work ethic, if you will — and you are undoubtedly seeing story, thinking story, planning it and writing more felicitously than you were before starting here. This is no time to idle for six months, or even six weeks, and let all that newly polished machinery start to rust again. You need to maintain a creative pace to keep what you've achieved so far, and to assure further growth.

Also, going ahead into a new project is the greatest guard you can have against possible discouragement if the first or even the first few publishers return the story you're about to mail. It's mighty tough out there today, and rejection is certainly possible. If this story is the only one you have worked on, and you have no current project going, a rejection can be devastating. But if you have other work going on, you can take the blow with less pain, get it back in the mail again, and return to the current work rather than lapsing into discouragement because *the only* story you care about just came back.

You'll also find that continuing on a new project will help you maintain the good work habits you may have built up at considerable cost of effort during your work through this book. Don't lose your work habits by allowing yourself a "vacation" that might extend for months. You work best when you continue working, maintaining creative momentum.

Finally, story ideas beget story ideas. When you're at work on a story, you're more open to other story ideas. At the same time, you'll find that everyday events or casual meetings with new people may become relevant to the story you have going right now . . . if you have a story going right now. I have often had the experience of seeing something or meeting someone or hearing a conversation that seemed almost divinely placed in my path, so perfectly did it fit into the story I was preoccupied with at that very moment. My experience indicates that you will be more alert to all kinds of fiction possibilities if you're working on something—and an amazing amount of material may seem instantly relevant to the current project.

It's as if your preoccupation with the story at hand puts everything in your life into a different focus—makes everything potentially relevant—keeps you incredibly alert for things that might somehow fit.

If there were no other reason to maintain a continuous writing schedule, this alone would be justification enough.

So I hope you will be thinking about the next project—maybe even sifting back through cards and creating new ones—as we look briefly at marketing this story so recently concluded.

## ABOUT AGENTS

An inevitable question at writers conferences: "Should I have an agent?"

The polite answer: Maybe.

The realistic answer: Unless you already have an agent, your chances of finding one today are virtually nil as long as you work only on the short story.

Another answer: If you already have an agent because you also do other kinds of writing, or have perhaps published a book-length collection of your short fiction — and if that agent seems to be trying on your behalf — stay with her.

All of this may sound like one of the great cop-outs of recent times, but the truth is that getting an agent in today's rough-and-tumble publishing world — if you're an unpublished author — is about as easy as salvaging a million in Spanish gold from a sunken ship in the Gulf of Mexico. It's a tough time in publishing right now, and agents — like many authors — are scrambling to make ends meet as markets dwindle, the "star system" prints mediocre stories by well-known writers rather than better ones by unknowns, print costs go up, circulation of many publications goes down, ad revenue shrinks, etc., etc.

Or to say this much more briefly: If you don't have an agent at present, it will be easier for you to sell your short fiction on your own than to find an agent with the time and guts to risk investing effort in you until you have a track record.

That, however, is OK. Many writers have sold stories "over the transom," with no agent and no introduction to an editor other than the story itself, mailed in. It's hard but not impossible.

Perhaps, of course, you feel you simply can't handle the paperwork and possible disappointment of seeing manuscripts come back, then checking a list of possible markets, sending it out again, and waiting again. Perhaps you believe you *must* have an agent.

If so, there are publications that list literary agents, and writers magazines often include advertisements from agencies looking for new talent. Most such agencies will charge a reading fee for the first manuscript they evaluate for you. This is to discourage people who are not serious, and to defray the costs of reading and then sending you a critique of your work. The better reading-fee agencies will credit your account with whatever you pay them for a reading, and then if (and when) they sell your story, they will deduct the fee from whatever they would ordinarily collect as their 10 or 15 percent commission.

There are a few agencies that sell little or nothing, and exist to collect reading fees. Reputable writers magazines do not carry ads from these crooks. Also, you may get further information by asking around at your local writers club. If all else fails and you still aren't sure about an agency, send them a letter asking to see a copy of their fee schedule and standard agent-client agreement. Then make up your mind from there.

Remember, though, that an agent is not necessary to sell copy, and your chances of finding one are slight at best. Plan to send in your own copy to the magazines. Only when you start to hit the really big markets such as *Playboy* or *The New Yorker* will your need for an agent as negotiator become serious, and by that time you'll be able to find one.

## FINDING THE APPROPRIATE MARKET

It would be lovely if one could scan the magazine racks, grab a few publications, study them, and send off a story with some sense of certainty about the story fitting that publication. Unfortunately, market analysis is an uncertain endeavor at best, and one that continues throughout a writer's life as publications change, editors change, readers change, you change, the times change.

If you followed the market analysis suggestions outlined in chapter fifteen as part of the revision process, you have already accomplished about as much as you can in terms of looking at a magazine and determining whether your latest story may fit that publication's preferences. But as suggested there, your study of published fiction should be an ongoing process; you may imagine that you have analyzed a certain magazine's contents until you know everything about it, but then as you continue to study it you might come up with some new insight that somehow earlier eluded you.

For example, I once knew a writer who studied a particular mystery magazine for more than a year before she was thunderstruck one evening to realize that the magazine had published more missing-persons stories than any other kind, month after month for well over a year. This writer's current story could easily be altered to feature a missing-person angle; she made the changes, sent in the story, and was featured in an issue soon thereafter as the editor's new talent "find."

The lesson here is obvious: Even though you have studied a magazine for some period of time, and perhaps even had rejections from it in the past, you may benefit by continuing to read every issue and make appropriate analyses—*and written notes*—over more time.

In addition, however, there are a few other things you can do to better your chances of publication.

Read what the editors say about their wishes. By all means, consult a copy of *Novel & Short Story Writer's Market*. You may find a copy of this book in your library, but if you are at all serious you will buy a copy and peruse it on a regular basis. This book lists valuable marketing tips as well as the names and addresses of almost 2,000 publishers. Here, too, you can find the most up-to-date information about what the editor says he likes in a story for his publication. If your story in no way fits what the editor says he likes, why waste time and postage sending the story to him?

Similarly, check out current copies of magazines for writers. Each month, the best of these contain small display ads which may provide a clue to the founding of a new publication or the needs of a current one. In addition, industry news is often published here; if a magazine needs a particular kind of story, or perhaps wants to announce some change in editorial philosophy, this is where you might get such information first.

Some writers groups publish newsletters with up-to-the-minute market tips. The monthly newsletter published in my own state, for example, sometimes is the very first to print marketing information; that's because the small publication is more simply printed than bigger magazines, and can therefore get to press faster with new "scoops." These usually consist of the actual words of an editor stating what she would like to see.

Next, see if your target magazine has a set of writers' guidelines, or what they sometimes call a "tip sheet." Some magazines have such things, and will send a copy to you if you ask and enclose a stamped, self-addressed envelope. These guidelines can be quite specific, getting down to such items as desired age of the viewpoint character, and desired locales. If the magazine has no such information available, all you've lost in trying is a couple of stamps.

Then, look for and talk to published writers in your area. You may find someone who is selling to precisely the kind of magazines you hope to reach. At worst, a fellow writer might offer some casual insight into the magazine's wishes that had not become clear to you. At best, your new friend may know an editor, or some way to give you a better chance of getting a reading there.

A caveat that should be stated here at once: Ninety-nine times out of a hundred, you should *not* ask your fellow writer to "put in a good word" for you at the publisher's office, or anything of that nature. When I am occasionally asked to do such a thing, either with an editor or an agent, I cringe and look for a way out. Why?

Several reasons. I am not in the business of pushing the work of other authors; my job is to write or instruct, not market. Also, I usually have no idea what one of my editors might be looking for *right now*, nor do I have up-to-date information on story inventory that may already be in her files. Finally, I simply hate to bother a busy editor with personal pleas of any kind, even if putting in a good word for someone might make me look—to them!—like a good guy.

It's also a good idea to attend one or more good writers conferences every year. At these one- to three-day events, editors and agents are often the featured speakers. You should attend their sessions and listen *carefully* to what they have to say. Often they will dwell a bit on horrible marketing mistakes and misjudgments writers have made with them. Write these down and don't commit a similar atrocity. If the editor has positive suggestions, *follow* them.

With luck, too, you might get a few minutes with a given editor or agent, one-on-one. If you have some specific questions, this might be the place to ask them. At worst you can carry a copy of a manuscript or two under your arm, wave them, and thus vividly illustrate that you're a producer, not a mere talker.

Will an editor read your manuscript during a conference? Almost surely not. She may—if you have a grand idea and can state it in less than a minute—give you a card with her address, for submission by mail at a later date. This can give your manuscript a direct route past the pile of totally unsolicited manuscripts already piled up on the office floor in New York.

You may, of course, go to a conference and be disappointed. The editors there may, by bad luck, all be of the type who won't have individual meetings at all. There are good conferences and bad ones.

How do you learn the difference? Ask fellow writers about conferences they have attended. Check the back ad pages of a magazine such as *Writer's Digest*, where a number of conferences are listed. Find the annual edition where brief information is printed on all the conferences the editors can track down. Write to the given address and ask for a copy of the conference brochure.

Whatever part of the country you live in, there is a good writers conference somewhere in reachable distance. My speaking engagements have taken me from coast to coast and from as far north as Minneapolis to as far south as Galveston. I've found excellent, well-planned, well-staffed meetings everywhere. Look for one of these.

Even if you're disappointed the first time, try again somewhere else. The market information you glean may be invaluable.

Finally, it goes without saying that you should read at least one national magazine for writers on a regular, subscribing basis.

## A FEW DREADFUL NO-NO'S

Just as there are some things you can do to help your chances, there are errors you can make which could doom your manuscript. Here is a sampling of those.

Don't telephone the editor. This is almost always a ghastly mistake. She's busy and hassled. She'll get to your manuscript as soon as she can. You're wasting her time—and marking yourself as an anxious amateur. Send your manuscript in properly and wait it out.

Don't ask in your covering letter for constructive criticism. If she really likes your work, and considers it a true near-miss, you'll likely hear from her in a letter. Otherwise, don't expect helpful advice. Again, the editor doesn't have time. Also, too many novices mistake helpful suggestions for an indication that the editor will buy the story if the advice is followed, when that may not be the case at all; once, for example, I had a student who got a nice bit of advice from a mystery editor to whom she had submitted a love story; she followed the advice and then pummelled the editor with multiple revisions—"following instructions"—for the kind of story the editor would never have bought under any circumstances because, while excellent, it was not the kind of story that magazine ever published.

Editors also hate to offer criticism, even if they happen to like the story and can find time to comment, because the advice sometimes helps someone else in the business, not their publication. In this regard (quite the opposite of the situation described just above) an editor wrote the author of a novel a long letter telling him how to revise the manuscript. Six months later, the editor got a letter from the author saying in effect, "I can never thank you enough for your help; I just sold the manuscript to your competitor."

Don't bombard the editor with repeated letters asking what's going on with the submission. This is almost as bad as telephoning, which I've already warned you about.

Don't submit a less-than-perfect manuscript. A manuscript with erasures, typos, smudges, wrong margins, etc., will likely never be pulled all the way out of your envelope before being tossed onto the rejection pile. If you can't make it *look* professional, why should an editor bother with you in the first place?

Don't send long letters of transmittal with the manuscript. At most, the editor might like to have a polite, short letter stating that you're hereby submitting a story titled such-and-such, and that you're qualified to write this story because you are a surgeon, just like the main character, or whatever. Almost anything else will mark you a bumbling amateur, and hurt your chances more than help them.

## CONTINUING YOUR SEARCH

As you probably already realize, none of the above information is going to make it a whole lot easier to place your new story. The commercial marketplace today is so tough that even seasoned pros sometimes almost despair. You must continue to research markets, analyze your own copy, and keep manuscripts in the mail. An entirely separate shoebox or filing box of market information cards may develop over time. The key here is to strive always to learn new things, and apply them in your submissions. The effort will pay off in the long run. And just as writing a new story gives you more than one item to hang your hat of faith on, continuing market research will give you additional knowledge that can give *this* story a better chance than any you might have sent out blindly in the past.

Here, however, one final word of caution. There are writers now and then who make such a "thing" of market research that they might become an agent more readily than a published writer. There are others who get so hung up on what an editor might want that they completely wreck their own style and betray their individuality in trying to "write a story to fit." In this, as in so many other aspects of writing—and life—you can't afford to let a good thing carry you away.

Your first job, after all, is another story.

Moderation is the key. That, and persistence.

## SUMMARY

Market research can improve your chances of finding a home for this latest story. Nothing can guarantee success in placing it, but learning more about your target publications can help a lot, and there are many good sources of information, including books, magazines, tip sheets and writers conferences.

How you submit the manuscript can have an impact on its likely success. There are things you should do, and things you shouldn't.

Market study is a lifelong job, but must never become such an obsession that your creative output is reduced, or you find that you have sold out totally in a last-ditch attempt to use all that you now know about a market . . . and write a story that will match perfectly even though it isn't you.

## Chapter Eighteen

# Charting Your Future

---

PROGRESS CHECK:

✔ *Is the story finished and in the mail?*

✔ *Are you ready to begin work on the next one?*

✔ *Do you plan to keep trying, even if you encounter discouraging setbacks?*

✔ *Have you continued to add observation cards and others, such as research information, to your growing arsenal of planning material?*

---

L ong ago, when I was just setting out to be a writer, I began to learn a bit about such things as good work habits, scene structure, characterization and dialogue devices. But I could not seem to put everything together into a single, coherent vision of what fiction was all about. I felt like I had many facts, but little total understanding.

I took my plaint to my writing coach, the late Dwight V. Swain.

"Work," he told me. "The synthesis will come. One day you'll look up and see how everything ties together, and you'll say, 'Good heavens, I *understand.*'"

"But what," I pressed, "do I do in the meantime when so much seems so complex to me, and I can't seem to grasp the big picture?"

Swain leaned back in his chair and smiled. "Trust the system," he told me.

It was some of the best advice ever given me. It's the advice I want to leave with you now, as we close this description of a systematic, hands-on approach to your work.

It may be that parts of the work you did in preparing your story for this book did not go as well as you had hoped. In spots you may have done some work that you considered irrelevant. Or you didn't understand why such work was called for.

In the months ahead, I hope you will continue to use this program, and remember Swain's advice to me so long ago: Trust the system.

It works.

I hope the Time Out sections have already put you on the road to a synthesis. But perhaps a final broad analysis of the system at this juncture will help turn on lights for you as you work to put everything together. Involved in everything we've looked at are the following major concepts.

1. A systematic approach to your work will pay dividends. That's why you were urged from the start to use a card-filing system for your analysis, research and writing.

2. Fiction is not real life, but your keen observation of real-life people and situations will sharpen your ability to recognize and tell good stories, and people them with vivid characters. Observations should be recorded on cards as quickly as possible, and retained in a system.

3. A writer's journal is more than a diary. It can record observations, your feelings as a writer, sketches, reports on your emotional state at any given time, financial records, hopes and dreams for the future, and anything else that may help you in the months and years to come.

4. The imagination can be made to work in a disciplined fashion. The Map provides a framework in which disciplined imaginative work can be done.

5. Stories are of three types: conflict, decision or discovery.

6. It is important to take a self-inventory to know what kinds of stories you like the best. Then you can plan to act accordingly.

7. Characters live by a self-concept and have traits that you can demonstrate with tags.

8. The structure of stories is one of scene and sequel.

9. Stories begin with change.

10. The story-opening change should develop into a character goal or need, which becomes the story question.

11. The ending of the story must answer the question.

12. Good setting is essential, and may require research. Cards can become the record of that research.

13. Good work habits are essential to the professional writer.

14. Story-planning cards should contain an outline for every

scene and sequel in the tale's sequence of events, even if the writer later decides not to "play" some of them.

15. Scene-sequel cards can easily be arranged into a visual diagram of the planned story.

16. First drafts may be frightening, but should be undertaken as soon as planning and research are finished.

17. The first draft should be written straight through, at "white heat," without undue regard for worries about rough spots or snags in plot or character.

18. To begin the revision process, the writer should allow a cooling-off period.

19. Revision should be done in several planned steps, from casual reading at first to a final verbal polishing.

20. Study of potential markets is a vital and career-long job.

## EXPANDING YOUR HORIZONS

We could, of course, expand this list into virtually another book. You will, in fact, find a more detailed, sequential checklist of principles and procedures in the appendix. But our business is almost done, and only a few additional observations need to be offered.

You should work continually to expand your creative horizons. Here are a couple of ways to work at that: (a) you can talk to friends about their preferences in fiction, and follow up by reading some of their favorites, and (b) you can study and work at stories of lengths other than your usual short-story wordage.

In this regard, you might want to interview a few friends. Ask them their favorite authors, publications and novels. Make notes on cards. Keep these, and as time permits, look up those favorites and read some of them.

At the same time, explore on your own. Go to the store and pick up a couple of unfamiliar magazines containing fiction, and read them to see what you've been missing. Go to the library (or better yet, from my standpoint, a bookstore!), and buy editions of several recent short-story anthologies, and study those.

Similarly, get into the habit of picking up popular novels, reading them, and marking the techniques and principles shown here in this book. You will be astounded at first, perhaps, to see how much more clearly you can now understand how the novelist uses techniques identical with those of the short story writer. This insight may make one idea or another clearer in your own mind, as it may apply to your work.

Try — even if casually — laying out a few general plot or character cards for a much longer story, a novella or even a novel. Sketch in your plans in big chunks of action and broad-brush strokes, just to practice thinking at a longer length. Don't get hung up on details. Be sure to keep all such cards filed under separate category, because one day you might decide to use them in a book-length.

Continue to visualize the kind of writing success you hope to attain, and make it a practice to write down something positive and optimistic in your journal at least once a week.

Don't give up on the system even if the first story or two meet rejection. Be sure to keep those manuscripts in the mail until *all* possible markets have been tried. In the meantime, realize that repeated use of the system in planning and executing other stories is probably making you much more facile and clear-headed in story-telling than you ever were before. This system guarantees continued orderly growth.

Work hard and steadily, but allow yourself time now and then for calm reflection.

And finally, maintain your hope as well as your expectations. Then one day I hope to be appearing at a writers conference somewhere, and meet you there as another speaker . . . a successful new author with all the confidence in the world, and wisdom to share with other seekers like you too were, not so long ago.

# APPENDIX
*A short checklist guide to principles and procedures*

On the following pages you will find a brief guide to ideas and procedures presented in this book. This condensed discussion of subjects is designed to provide you with an overview of the methodology used in this book.

Topics might have been arranged alphabetically, as is usually done in the conventional index. But that would have meant listing them out of the order in which they were presented in this book, and usually out of the order in which tasks should be undertaken. This would have been entirely out of the logical, orderly spirit of our approach to writing.

In addition, arrangement by alphabetical order would require a topical, factual arrangement rather than the question method used as frequently as possible in the following pages; the question system allows the writer to use the appendix as a master storytelling checklist.

Thus the following items are arranged in the sequence they were presented in the book, chapter by chapter, and in self-check question form when possible. If you note a particular principle or procedure you wish to review, it will be easy to refer back to the parent chapter.

## CHAPTER ONE

☐ Have you begun to avoid the trap of writing by inspiration alone? That's seldom a path to a consistent, successful creative career.

☐ Are you beginning to appreciate the need for a logical work *system* in your craft? There is no problem in writing that a logical approach won't help you solve.

☐ The writer must do the assignments as directed, in the order assigned. Are you being careful to follow these instructions? Any time you fall into confusion, backtrack to the principle or assignment that seems to have dropped out of memory.

☐ Are you making sure to be patient, and working step by step? The old saw, "Haste makes waste," applies here. Take your time!

## CHAPTER TWO

- ☐ Have you procured a good supply of 3″×5″ or 4″×6″ filing-type cards? These are essential.
- ☐ Are you carrying cards with you to record observations or ideas as soon as they come along?
- ☐ A set of colored pencils will help you mark up copy later. These should be on hand now, along with two spiral-type notebooks.
- ☐ Do you have a definite work schedule set up?
- ☐ Have you set up a regular workplace—an office or corner somewhere?

## CHAPTER THREE

- ☐ You need to have in your filing system ten cards listing things you feel strongly about. Do you have at least that many as part of your self-inventory?
- ☐ Do you have five cards mentioning an event that aroused strong emotion in you?
- ☐ Five cards listing an idea or concept in which you believe most deeply?
- ☐ Five that list an activity you enjoy?
- ☐ Five listing an activity you detest?
- ☐ Do you have at least one card describing briefly, but in complete sentences, some event or activity in your past that brought you great happiness?
- ☐ Another card similarly listing an event that brought you great sadness?
- ☐ Another describing an event that made you very angry?
- ☐ Another describing an event that frightened you?
- ☐ Do you have all these cards filed in a box under a major category such as "self-inventory," and under subcategories such as "angry event"?
- ☐ Have you re-read these cards and tried to determine—if the cards were shown to you as a description of a stranger—what kind of person you would conclude that stranger to be?
- ☐ Have you examined some of your recent fiction to see if it was about some of the things you really feel strongly about?
- ☐ Have you marked up some of your own copy, using a different colored pencil to identify different emotions mentioned therein? Have you studied the markups to see if you can determine any characteristic pattern in your own work?

☐ Have you recorded observations about your own tendencies in your journal?

☐ Have you analyzed one or more of your favorite magazines in terms of characteristic length, setting, style? Have you *recorded* all such observations in cards for that publication?

☐ Have you given additional analytical study to a favorite author?

## CHAPTER FOUR

☐ Do you have a growing collection of character cards that describe personality traits you find appealing?

☐ Do your cards in this category provide more specificity in saying what you mean by a particular trait, such as "kindness"?

☐ Do you have at least twenty character cards outlining traits you find undesirable?

☐ The traits outlined on your cards are abstract. You should also have listings of tags that will concretely illustrate the traits to your reader. Do you have those? This is another aspect of planning on which you should work continually, over months and years.

☐ Exaggeration has great value in fiction character. Are your tags and traits exaggerated enough?

## CHAPTER FIVE

☐ You should understand the three basic types of story. What are they?

☐ Are you sure you clearly understand the difference between conflict and adversity? Why is this understanding vital?

☐ Have you filled out at least three cards for each kind of story, outlining a tale you might tell of this type?

☐ Have you studied and categorized some of your own fiction to determine what your own natural storytelling tendency must be?

☐ In a story of conflict, what will likely be some of the dominant traits of the lead character?

☐ The same question for a story of decision.

☐ The same question for a story of discovery.

☐ Do you have a collection of character objective cards that has grown beyond the ten assigned here?

☐ Do you know why such objectives are essential to the character's happiness?

☐ Have you followed essentially the same process for the other types of stories?

☐ Is there a perhaps-lengthy entry in your journal, recording what you may have discovered about yourself through the work on these character and story cards?

## CHAPTER SIX

☐ Is your collection of observation cards — telling descriptions of real people — constantly growing?

☐ Does each such card clearly define that person's dominant impression?

☐ Are you carrying appearance cards with you on a regular basis?

☐ Are you observing how real people talk? And making notes on cards?

☐ Do you understand how to condense real-life dialogue to make it read faster? And why you must do this? Have you practiced?

☐ How can dialogue in a story become "too realistic?"

☐ Have you marked up some of your own copy to make sure you aren't using dialogue as an author convenience?

☐ Have you red-penciled some of your own work, killing speech-making?

## CHAPTER SEVEN

☐ Where does your current story take place? Do you know *everything* you need to know about that setting?

☐ If there are things you still need to know about the setting, what steps are you taking to learn them?

☐ Do your characters fit the setting, and vice versa?

☐ Does your plot dovetail with both setting and characters?

☐ Do you have a growing collection of factual cards concerning various possible settings for future stories? This is the kind of work that can be done "between stories," as when you are letting a manuscript cool before revising it.

☐ What are some of the best local sources of research data?

☐ Have you practiced description by direct method, by simile and by metaphor?

☐ Do you have setting-orientation cards in a separate file category?

☐ Have you analyzed some of your own copy to see your tendencies in handling setting, and if you have found anything wanting,

what steps are you taking to strengthen your work in this con-
nection?

## CHAPTER EIGHT

☐ Are you continuing to work in logical ways, straight through the
story from front to back, doing the assigned tasks?

☐ Have you used the short checklist in this chapter to make sure
you have the answers to many central story questions?

☐ Do you know the kind of story it is to be, generally?

☐ Have you decided how it is to start?

☐ How it is to end?

☐ Who is your viewpoint character? Why?

## CHAPTER NINE

☐ Make sure all decisions made to date are as specific and concrete
as possible. Search for vague generalities about such matters as
story type or character motive. If you find such generalities,
sharpen them and make them more specific.

☐ Are the protagonist's motives clear?

☐ The antagonist's?

☐ After intense planning, most writers lay out their scene and transition cards in the order they imagine (at this point) the story
playing out — even if some of the cards may wind up happening
offstage, and never being actually narrated in the story "now."
Are you ready to take this step before moving on? Have you
done so?

## CHAPTER TEN

☐ The story character's dominant impression is so vital that you
should consider it further, and try to sharpen it, before moving
on.

☐ Have you reviewed earlier trait and tag cards, expanding some
of the tags into meaningful clusters?

☐ Characters in the same story must contrast with one another —
physically, emotionally, intellectually — if each is to appear as
vivid as possible. Have you checked your work to date for this
need, and sharpened characters who need to stand out from the
rest of the cast?

☐ Have you used colored pencils to look for contrast markers in
published copy, and in your own?

☐ Have you clearly ranked the people in your story in terms of relative importance?

☐ Is the *role* to be assigned to each character clear in your mind?

☐ Why is the self-concept vital to good characterization?

☐ Have you clearly defined on cards the self-concept of each major player in your story plan?

☐ Does the motive of each character grow out of the self-concept, as it should?

## CHAPTER ELEVEN

☐ In the story you now have under way, what is the story question?

☐ Does the story question relate directly to the character's self-concept and desire for happiness?

☐ Can your story question be provided with a definite answer?

☐ Does your planned story opening plant the story question for the reader?

☐ Does the ending clearly answer the question the story raised?

☐ Do your story cards contain related story questions and answers, perhaps not only for the current story, but for possible others?

☐ As we delve more deeply into the nature of scene and sequel, are you perfectly clear in your mind what the structure of scene is? Of sequel? How they tie together?

☐ Do you have cards for every scene and sequel, perhaps going back and changing or adding to the scene and transition cards planned earlier?

☐ Does the length of scene and sequel jibe with the general type of story you plan to tell?

☐ Have you planned each scene with specified goal, conflict and disaster?

☐ Have you planned every sequel with its component parts specified, even if you don't plan to use some of them in the finished script?

☐ Do your scenes move the story forward by ending badly for the central character?

☐ Do your sequels show the character's reaction to what just took place, and then get the character into the next scene?

☐ Make sure you have a scene and sequel card for every bit of your story.

☐ Have you tested your scene-sequel layout against desired length and pace of story?

## CHAPTER TWELVE

- ☐ Have you examined your laid-out scene-sequel cards and then reviewed your earlier self-inventory cards? Are you still sure about the kind of story you want to write . . . and writing out of your sincere feelings?
- ☐ It's time to arrange character trait and tag cards under the scenes or sequels where such characters will first enter the story.
- ☐ Have you fleshed out the characters?
- ☐ Have you arrayed setting data cards where you believe you can use their contents in the story?
- ☐ Do you have a detailed climax/ending card filled out and placed at the end of your card array?
- ☐ Is the ending the most dramatic possible?
- ☐ Does it clearly answer the story question?
- ☐ Have you come up with a clearer idea of the timing of the story, what you will tell and what you may condense or elide, and how all these decisions will affect story length, likely readership, and your own tendencies as a writer at this point in your development?

## CHAPTER THIRTEEN

- ☐ Are you conquering fears, and determined to write the first draft straight through, start to finish, without big lapses away from the word processor?
- ☐ Does an important *change* start your story? Could you devise such a change to help the story get started?
- ☐ Does your opening establish personal threat?
- ☐ Does the story continue to move forward in an inexorable way?
- ☐ Are you maintaining a regular production schedule?
- ☐ Are you making sure to do some things likely to relax you and enhance your physical well-being, such as healthy exercise and relaxation?
- ☐ Make sure your story does not make life impossible for the viewpoint character.

## CHAPTER FOURTEEN

- ☐ Are you keeping quiet about the story while writing the first draft? Don't talk it out of your system!
- ☐ Remember that asking for advice at this juncture will only bring you grief and confusion ninety-nine times out of a hundred.

☐ Don't take it to the writers club.

☐ Try not to worry about the story's eventual acceptability. One thing at a time.

☐ Are you getting new plot ideas as you write? Are you being sure to reject them for *this* story, while noting them on cards for some other one?

☐ Do you have at least three cards filled out with observations or statements of faith which can sustain you through inevitable uncertainty and self-doubt during first draft?

## CHAPTER FIFTEEN

☐ Have you finished your rough draft before worrying about revising? You should have a complete draft in the box before thinking about fixes, even obvious ones.

☐ Remember that revision is a multiple-step process. Do you plan to go through the manuscript a number of times, recognizing that you can't possibly spot everything on a single pass?

☐ The first step is repairing or changing things you realized might need attention even as you wrote the rough draft and forged ahead at high speed despite the apparent problem. Have you made marginal notes, pasted in any note cards or slips of paper calling for some revision already apparent?

☐ Similarly, have you marked with colored pencil or roughly written in any obviously needed corrections that you happened to notice while doing the "rough carpentry work" mentioned above?

☐ Are you convinced of the need for a cooling-off period before further revision? Make a list of the things you plan to do while trying *not* to think about the story in your desk drawer.

☐ You may wish to do some further market research during the cooling period. Have you picked out more issues of a magazine or two?

☐ Do you have market cards listing such items as apparent target audience, story lengths and characteristic settings, kinds of story people usually portrayed, usual amount of dialogue?

☐ Have you copied a few pages out of a favorite story in a favored magazine, then made comparisons between the appearance of these pages and the kind of manuscript page you usually wind up with?

☐ Have you done some checking on grammar and syntax—word

lengths, sentence lengths, typical paragraph construction?

☐ Have you, in addition to making more market cards, tried your hardest to crystallize conclusions you might draw about your own tendencies as a writer at this point? *Have you entered these in your journal?*

## CHAPTER SIXTEEN

☐ Make sure that at least a week has passed since you last looked at your first-draft manuscript.

☐ Do you understand how to do a first "casual" reading? Have you done that in the right order?

☐ Have you carefully noted any major revision needs that you might have discovered during your "casual" reading?

☐ Have you made correction cards, stick-on papers or marginal notes that you can later copy into the manuscript?

☐ It's time to check grammar and spelling much more carefully. This work may be tedious, but are you sure you've done it meticulously?

☐ Have you looked for such abominations as purple prose and ruthlessly eliminated it; have you simplified the language in every way you can imagine?

☐ Having gotten this far in revision, you may wish to print out a new copy. Did you decide to keyboard in all corrections noted so far, and give yourself a clean second draft at this point?

☐ Are you going through the clean copy, using a checklist such as the one outlined in this chapter, to look for potential problems with such matters as story or character background, stated plot intentions, character names that may sound or look alike, proper exaggeration of major story people, self-concept, sufficient physical description, consistency of viewpoint, clarity of story question (one more check on this!), and all the other items that may be on your own checklist as derived from this chapter and your self-analysis?

☐ Is there *anything* you might have forgotten or overlooked?

☐ It's time at last to make a final, corrected printout.

☐ Will you give the final printout two or three days, at least, for an additional cool-down period?

☐ In a final, detailed, critical read-through, have you detected anything else you might want to fix? Remember all the work you have done, and have confidence. As stated before, don't fall prey to crippling self-doubt at this late stage. It's normal to feel a little sick of the whole thing at this point.

## CHAPTER SEVENTEEN

☐ Are you beginning to plan your next story?

☐ Are you determined to keep this latest story in the mail to appropriate potential markets, even if today's conditions have made it impossible right now to take on a literary agent?

☐ Is your market research ongoing, with such aids as market publications and additional copies of newly discovered magazines?

☐ Have you looked for possible tip sheets?

☐ Have you talked with published writers in your area?

☐ Have you begun to seek out one or more writers conferences that could open doors for you?

☐ Is your subscription current for at least one national writers magazine?

☐ Have you checked out any regional writers groups that might have newsletters that could contain marketing information?

☐ Are you familiar with some of the dreadful, amateurish submission mistakes listed in this chapter, and resolved not to make them?

☐ While continuing market research, are you being careful not to let it become such an obsession that it interferes with your creative output?

## CHAPTER EIGHTEEN

☐ Are you ready to trust the Map process over the long haul?

☐ Have you continued to observe real-life people and situations and recorded them on your cards?

☐ Are you maintaining a creative record and observations in your journal?

☐ Have you thoughtfully re-read the short list of observations about the future as contained in this chapter?

☐ Are you working to expand your horizons by meeting new people, seeing new places, reading different kinds of stories, including those of vastly different length?

☐ Will you maintain your faith, knowing that you can't be beaten unless you give up?

# INDEX

# *More Great Books for Writers!*

**1998 Novel & Short Story Writer's Market**—Discover thousands of fiction writing opportunities. You'll find all the facts vital to the success of your writing career, including an up-to-date listing of buyers of books, articles and stories, listings of contests and awards, plus articles and interviews with top professionals. *#10525/$22.99/656 pages/paperback*

**20 Master Plots (And How to Build Them)**—Write great contemporary fiction from timeless plots. This guide outlines 20 plots from various genres and illustrates how to adapt them into your own fiction. *#10366/$17.99/240 pages*

**Handbook of Short Story Writing, Volume II**—Orson Scott Card, Dwight V. Swain, Kit Reed and other noted authors bring you sound advice and timeless techniques for every aspect of the writing process. *#10239/$13.99/252 pages/paperback*

**Fiction Writer's Workshop**—Explore each aspect of the art of fiction including point of view, description, revision, voice and more. At the end of each chapter you'll find more than a dozen writing exercises to help you put what you've learned into action. *#48033/$14.99/256 pages/paperback*

**Creating Characters: How to Build Story People**—Grab the empathy of your reader with characters so real they'll jump off the page. You'll discover how to make characters come alive with vibrant emotion, quirky personality traits, inspiring heroism, tragic weaknesses and other uniquely human qualities. *#10417/$14.99/192 pages/paperback*

**Writing the Blockbuster Novel**—Let a top-flight agent show you how to weave the essential elements of a blockbuster into your own novels with memorable characters, exotic settings, clashing conflicts and more! *#10393/$18.99/224 pages*

**The Art and Craft of Novel Writing**—Using examples from classic and contemporary writers ranging from John Steinbeck to Joyce Carol Oates, Hall guides you through the process of crafting a novel. In example-packed discussions, Hall shows what works and why. *#48002/$14.99/240 pages/paperback*

**The Writer's Guide to Everyday Life in the Middle Ages**—This time-travel companion will guide you through the medieval world of Northwestern Europe. Discover the facts on dining habits, clothing, armor, festivals, religious orders and much more—everything you need to paint an authentic picture. *#10423/$17.99/256 pages*

**The Writer's Guide to Everyday Life from Prohibition through World War II**—Uncover all the details you need to add color, depth and a ring-of-truth to your work. You'll find an intimate look at what life was like back then, including popular slang, the Prohibition, the Depression, World War II, crime, transportation, fashion, radio, music and much more! *#10450/$18.99/272 pages*

**Police Procedural: A Writer's Guide to the Police and How They Work**—Learn how police officers work, when they work, what they wear, who they report to, and how they go about controlling and investigating crime. *#10374/$16.99/272 pages/paperback*

**Private Eyes: A Writer's Guide to Private Investigators**—How do people become investigators? What procedures do they use and what tricks/tactics? This guide gives you the "inside scoop" on the world of private eyes! *#10373/$15.99/208 pages/paperback*

**Scene of the Crime: A Writer's Guide to Crime-Scene Investigation**—Save time with this quick reference book! You'll find loads of facts and details on how police scour crime scenes for tell-tale clues. *#10319/$15.99/240 pages/paperback*

**The Fiction Dictionary**—Discover genres you've never attempted, writing devices you'll want to explore, and fresh characters to populate your stories through full, vivid descriptions, and lively examples from classic and contemporary fiction. *#48008/$18.99/336 pages*

**The Best Writing on Writing, Volume 2**—This year's best collection of memorable essays, book excerpts and lectures on fiction, nonfiction, poetry, screenwriting and the writing life. *#48013/$16.99/224 pages/paperback*

**The Writer's Digest Character Naming Sourcebook**—Forget the guesswork! Twenty thousand first and last names (and their meanings) from around the world will help you pick the perfect name to reflect your character's role, place in history and ethnicity. *#10390/$18.99/352 pages*

**The Writer's Digest Guide to Manuscript Formats**—Don't take chances with your hard work! Learn how to prepare and submit books, poems, scripts, stories and more with the professional look editors expect from a good writer. *#10025/$19.99/200 pages*

**Turning Life Into Fiction**—Your life, those of your friends and family members, newspaper accounts, conversations overheard—these can be the bases for novels and short stories. Here, Robin Hemley shows how to make true stories even better. You'll learn how to turn journal entries into fiction; identify memories that can be developed; and fictionalize other people's stories. Exercises help you hone your writing skills. *#40829/ $14.99/208 pages/paperback*

**Description**—Discover how to use detailed description to awaken the reader's senses; advance the story using only relevant description; create original word depictions of people, animals, places, weather and much more! *#10451/$15.99/176 pages*

**38 Most Common Fiction Writing Mistakes**—Take steps to diagnose and correct the 38 most common fiction writing land mines that can turn dynamite story ideas into slush pile rejects. *#10528/$12.99/128 pages/paperback*

**Voice & Style**—Discover how to create character and story voices! You'll learn to write with a spellbinding narrative voice, create original character voices, write dialogue that conveys personality, control tone of voice to create mood and make the story's voices harmonize into a solid style. *#10452/$15.99/176 pages*

**Setting**—Don't ignore setting as a key to powerful, moving fiction. Bickham, author of over 80 published novels, demonstrates how to use sensual detail and vivid language to paint the perfect setting for your story. *#10397/$14.99/176 pages*

**You Can Get Published**—The principles of writing for publication delivered in short, easy-to-master steps. Writers will discover how to spark great story ideas and generate reader interest by writing short fillers, light verse, epigrams and more. *#10546/$12.99/ 128 pages/paperback*

**You Can Write Children's Books**—First time children's writers will learn to follow the important writing and submission guidelines they need to get their work in print, including hot trends and manuscript attention-getting tips. *#10547/$12.99/128 pages/ paperback*